~~~p on that Corn

Job to Boss:
Starting a Business
from Scratch

Endorsements

"Melanie has produced a significant addition to the resources available for people transiting from being employed to being their own boss. As someone who has taught this subject to a wide variety of health professionals for around 30 years, I am of the opinion that this book - written from personal experience and research - should be a comprehensive support tool for readers. I am sure it will inspire, inform and encourage many to start and continue this challenging, but infinitely rewarding journey of self development and autonomy, underpinned by the exploration of our potential for change and growth."

David Balen, Chairman: Balens Specialist Insurance Brokers

"This is an interesting read if you look to switch from being in a job to becoming an entrepreneur and like to be aware of fears, concerns and to dos. And, you get reminded of the need to comply with GDPR as well."

Punit Bhatia, CEO and Data Protection Expert, Fit4Privacy

"If you are fed-up working for someone else and toying with starting your own business, then you must read this book. I wish I had this book when starting out as I knew nothing about running my own business, having passion for what you do is not enough, it would have saved me a long hard struggle and given me a great foundation to make the transition to self employed."

Penny Briant, Relationship Coach, Penny Your Coach

"Melanie Smith-Rawlings is an inspirational woman who has been there, done it and got the tee shirt.

She has overcome adversity and is a role model for anyone who struggles with that Sunday feeling of dread, hoping that

Monday morning never comes.

Melanie encourages us to think about what we have to offer which is of value to others that we would actually love to do instead. She takes us on a journey through the practicalities of achieving our dreams through asking a series of questions:

Do we have a reason? A Plan? The expertise? Who can help us, and the wisdom of learning from others. The book stresses the importance of acquiring and practising good habits which will help us reach our goals. This includes the importance of physical and mental health, and the mindset required to overcome fear and negativity to become who we are meant to be.

Step on That Corn is a step by step guide and kick up the rear (in a good way), if you want more from life and to turn your dreams into reality. I wholly recommend it."

Tony Brown, Founder and Director,
Total Body Health Ltd

"So many people will tell anyone who will listen, "I want to start my own business one day." Very few of us actually take that step, let alone write such an inspiring book on the subject, in order to encourage others to do the same. Rather than sugar coating the decision to 'go it alone', Melanie gives a very balanced picture sharing the lowest of lows, as well as the highest of highs. By sharing experiences so openly, honestly and vulnerably, Melanie allows us to learn from her wisdom rather than experience the same costly mistakes ourselves. Thank you Melanie for such a helpful, educational and entertaining read."

Roger Cheetham, Multi-award-winning International Speaker and Resilience Coach, Author
Mental Health Advocate

Melanie demonstrates the vital essentials in making self-employment work – passion, positivity and knowing your business. Many fear the change from guaranteed wage to the seeming insecurity of self-employment, but most that have made the change will tell you that it is the best thing they have ever done. The most frequent thing that we hear at the College is '...I wish I had discovered it ten years earlier'. Self-employment allows you to live the lifestyle that you wish. It's not simply about income – rather it's about freedom to work when you want to work, having control over your life/work balance, and doing it your way.

Melanie's experience is generously shared, informative and inspirational and should be essential reading for those who seek personal determination and fulfilment.

**John Falkner-Heylings BSc(Podiatric Medicine),
DipPodM, FPSPract, Podiatrist. Principal,
Senior Lecturer, Director of Clinical Studies,
The College of Foot Health Practitioners**

I was delighted and honoured when Melanie asked me to write a few words of endorsement for this fabulous book. Melanie has been like a flower growing, unfolding and blooming before my very eyes. In my humble view, a key and non-negotiable ingredient to running any successful business is passion. Melanie has passion for her business in bucket loads. Add to that, her investment in personal development and business training and you are witnessing the result. I'm truly chuffed to bits for you Melanie.

Readers will enjoy reading your journey and you will inspire many to step forward into their own power and start their own enterprise.

**Elaine Godley MBA, O.A. Dip (Psych),
Multiple Amazon #1 best selling author
and Perfect 10 VIP Health Mentor.**

Step on that Corn

Job to Boss:
Starting a Business from Scratch

Publications

Please leave a positive review on the Amazon Book Site, this makes a big difference and will help the book to gain more ratings.

Thank you.

Melanie.

Dedication

This book is dedicated to my late parents

Dolores and Ivor Smith.

I don't know what they would have thought of me leaving a job and starting a business, let alone writing a book about it, but in many ways both things happened in part because of them.

The picture below was taken at my wedding in 2005.

Interested People - Keep in Contact!

Melanie would love to hear from you and know about your Starting your own business journey. Feel free to contact her - full details are at the back of the book.

Meanwhile, it would be immensely useful if you could spare the time to give a review on Amazon. This book can help many struggling to start their business for the first time and your review could help them to seek out the right advice before starting, give them confidence to step on that corn and do it and not make costly mistakes! By giving a review not only will it help them but it will be great encouragement to Melanie too!

The QR code gives you access to extra resources from this book.

Contents

Preface: My Beginning

On Wednesday 17th January 2018 I shared this post on my social media along with the quote from Oprah Winfrey.

"I believe you have to make things happen because if you don't you will always live in regret. I started my business because I believed it would give me the chance for personal freedom, the chance to take responsibility for my life and my development, the chance to make something better for myself and other people.

If you don't believe you can do something you will never try and never do anything about the rut you are in, or the things which bother you.

My business has started small and there are people out there who are far smarter, cleverer, have better business sense and acumen than me, and have gone way past what I have achieved so far with my business.

Does this stop me from trying? You can't compare yourself to the successes of others. You can admire them and try to learn from them for sure. You can look at what you are doing and ask yourself what can I change to make this work better?

Just because you think you're failing doesn't mean you are. It simply means you need to accept where you are right now and do everything you can tomorrow and the next day to put yourself where you truly want to be."

I wrote this post after leaving my job of 17 years with Leicestershire Police as a member of the Support Staff and it was a massive step for me. I was reminded of this post, when it appeared in my feed recently, everything it says is still true and still resonates even though myself and the business have moved on. I'm still striving to do better, to learn more, and to keep on moving forward.

Introduction: My 'Why?'

Have you ever thought you might like to start a business? There are lots of reasons why you may be thinking about it or why you've already done so. Maybe you want to have more freedom in your life, to do what you want to do, on your terms and no one else's; to go where you want to go and to make the decisions which you want to make without somebody looking over your shoulder telling you what to do. You have an idea and vision about having your own business; it is easy or you'll make lots of money. The problem is you have little or no experience and knowledge about business.

Business is organic with changes and challenges through the seasons and if you're a business owner they're the things you're going to have to stand and face up to. Yes, you can make money, and yes you could even be financially free, but it isn't necessarily the easy ride you think it is.

Perhaps you were brought up being told you should get yourself good qualifications and then you'll get yourself a good job in which you'll be working most of your adult life. Or maybe qualifications and schooling wasn't your strength so you learnt a trade or you've worked for someone else plying your skills and knowledge which have been developed and learned on the job and perhaps you gained qualifications along the way.

You are A. N. Employee, and for whatever reason being an employee in what you do or where you work is unsatisfactory to you. Your stress levels rise as soon as you walk out the door to go to work and every day is the same.

A Massive Step

You return home at the end of the day tired and exhausted.

For years and years and years (17 in fact) I was working in a job I hated, with people I didn't much like and didn't much like me, wondering to myself, "What on earth am I doing here?"

There was no job satisfaction, no fun, and certainly no enjoyment. It was a drudgery going into a dark room with disgruntled people sitting there moaning and groaning doing jobs which none of them enjoyed doing. There didn't seem to be any purpose or point to the repetitive tasks; nobody ever gave any praise for the work done no matter how hard the effort nor were you made to you feel your contribution mattered.

- Perhaps you can relate to the above points?
- Do you go to work where each day is like the day before and the next day will be like the day you've just had?
- When you look at it and think about it, how much longer can you go on like this? or What is the point of you being there?

If you don't think you're fulfilling a purpose, but only going through the motions, this is exactly what you're doing.

> **You want to do something in your life**
>
> **which makes you feel rewarded.**

You do what makes other people happy, what's expected of you, but deep down it isn't you. You don't know how to change the dialogue and be the person you want to be or to do what you want to do. You know you want to do something different. You know you want to do something in your life which makes you feel rewarded as a human being and as a person. You know you want to do something which gives satisfaction to you so you can meaningfully impact the people you encounter along the way.

Finding Fulfilment

It's important to be fulfilled by what you do because wouldn't it be silly to give up the JOB and then start a business which weighs you down with even more worries and stress?

If you have already started in a business having come out of a job, as I did, then you'll find there is a load of things you never even knew or thought about. You may find your mindset will change because if you don't change how you think from being A. N. Employee to a Business Owner, you will find the transition hard and confusing. You may even end up right back where you started, finding yourself another job, or worse still returning to the same old job you left.

> ## 20% of businesses are likely to fail
>
> ## in their first year.

In 2021 64% of the UK workforce was keen to set up a business, but the statistics show 20% of businesses are likely to fail in their first year while around 60% will go bust within the first three.

The truth is, while there are many success stories, there are many who couldn't make it and you don't want this to be you.

Finding the Right Information for You

There are lots of books you could look at and read, but to be honest most of them I don't relate to. Do you know why? Most of the books I've been recommended to read have been written by men who are recommending the books by other men who they admire and are predominantly aimed at men. If you don't relate to the titles or authors would you pick them up? There are lots of amazing women out there who have written some very useful books, but business books seem to be dominated by men in my opinion.

The books you are told you must read seem to be by written by business owners who appear to be hugely successful people, they're very wealthy, have a fabulous lifestyle, the perfect kids, the big mansions, holiday homes, the fancy cars and designer labels on their clothes. They travel the world talking about what they do and everyone is in awe of them and the success they have created. You look at them and think they are very different from the person you are right now.

It may surprise you to learn, of entrepreneurs in the UK, only 1 in 3 are female and at least 20% start a business out of necessity and in terms of scaling and starting their business, women seem to be a lot less confident than men. It's no surprise then those women have a quieter voice when it comes to sharing their success.

If you look at the different business categories on Amazon, the top 100 books are dominated by men. And yes, there are books out there by women, but their voice isn't getting heard because the men have the market.

To be honest, I don't know everything about business. You can go out buy all of those recommended books, listen to different podcasts, and be confused with countless opinions. You can do 101 things on top of this if there's extra information you need and there's sure to be plenty more you can learn and find out for yourself.

> **The best place to start**
>
> **is to walk alongside someone**
>
> **who has been where you are right now.**

Maybe this will open you up to the possibilities about business and some things you should and could be doing right from the word go. Sometimes, the best place to start is to walk alongside someone who has been where you are

Business Owner

right now and who understands how it feels to be that person who knows and remembers vividly how it was to work the proverbial *"nine to five,"* earning a salary to pay the bills.

What are your reasons to step out in business?

There are countless reasons why you could be looking to start your own business, more often than not, for ordinary people who take this step to start a business, it is from a change which wasn't of your own making. A change of circumstances means you've had to find something new, to create an income stream which fits around the life changes with which you have to deal with right now.

Perhaps you thought working in a job you were set for life, therefore, any kind of change can be very disconcerting. You could be facing redundancy or the threat of redundancy, having to cut back your work hours for whatever reason. You could be the main carer to a family member which will impact you and the life you currently have. Perhaps you want to work more flexible hours or your health has been suffering because of your current job, working conditions, or situation.

> I started my own business as a Foot Health Practitioner (FHP) for health reasons and a distinct lack of job satisfaction. I had faced redundancy at least four times in the space of 5 years in what was supposed to be at a secure job environment as support staff with the police. The career development was rubbish and I was deeply unhappy. I spent months off work with ill health due to the work situation so I understand the challenges you may be going through right now and face at home, at work, or both.

You may be thinking you want to start your own business because you see it as a way out; the path to freedom. After you read this book, you will have help to think differently about being a business person and taking the first steps to start and to grow your own business which you can run alongside your life, if it is the right thing for you to do.

> **It can take years of dedication and hard work to get it right.**

I want this book to bring lots of questions and thoughts into your mind which haven't been there before. In fact, the more questions you ask yourself the more you will realise where the areas are which you need more knowledge on. This will give you an idea of some of the systems and processes you need to set up and things you can do. May this book inspire you to create a successful and happy business which is fulfilling and provides you with an income to support yourself and your family.

People often think when you have your own business, success and a big flow of cash happens quickly. In reality, and back on planet earth, few businesses are like this. It can take years of dedication and hard work to get it right. You may not appreciate the minutiae of running a business especially if you've not had any previous experience. There can be a steep learning curve unless you are already transferring over existing relevant skill sets. How big or small your business is doesn't matter so long as it creates the lifestyle you desire. What matters is what you do makes you happy, gives you satisfaction and enjoyment. Even when there are challenges you have to solve, you know you've achieved something worthwhile.

What I found from my own business and observing other people in theirs is there are some simple things you can learn and know which will help make the process of having and running your own business easier and more effective.

If you don't know where to start and wonder if the challenge of having a business is right for you, then this book is for you. This is to help you to take those very first steps with your business and to share knowledge I've discovered so far on my 'starting a business' journey.

1: Perceptive People Know Change Will Be Better

If you want to start a business, you need to be really clear on your *'why'*. What is your reason for starting a business? What do you hope to achieve through having your own business? Note, if you don't enjoy your current lifestyle or are unhappy in what you're doing right now, running a business won't necessarily solve these issues.

Advice from Entrepreneurs

I asked a group of entrepreneurs what advice would they give to someone planning to leave the 9–5 to start their own business. Here are some of their answers:

- Delegate tasks (if you can afford to) so you can focus on getting clients e.g., outsource admin to a VA (Virtual Assistant).
- Compartmentalise your diary and focus on Key Results Areas (KRAs) and Income Generating Tasks (IGTs).
- Get used to working in your own time.
- Have a passion for your new business.
- Have a clear business plan with actions and timescales and be prepared to adapt it with a contingency for unforeseen situations.
- Get used to failing and learn from your mistakes.
- Be patient.
- Network often and make new connections consistently every day.

- Start in your spare time while doing the 9 – 5 to prove the concept works and you have enough money to cover your costs with 6 months to 2 years worth of cash in the bank to cover living expenses.
- Watch and learn from the business world.
- Surround yourself with good quality entrepreneurs who are succeeding.
- Ask for help/advice from existing business owners.
- Have a focus, you may have to do stuff you don't like.
- Be passionate and self-driven, prepared for hard work, late nights, and self-doubt.
- Understand why you are doing it, make a list of your whys, so when you hit a wall you have them to remind you.
- Value and encourage new ideas.
- Reduce your overheads, minimise costs and stop any unnecessary expenditures such as holidays, etc.
- Don't think it's the easier option.
- Don't be afraid to say no and know your worth.
- Have clients/customers lined up.
- Hone your service, know your niche problem and the solution for it.
- Separate work from home.
- Balance research to taking action. Too much research and nothing gets done, too much action with no research and you could be going in the wrong direction.
- Have a financial freedom figure to work towards.
- Practice the skills which matter.
- Engage a reputable mentor.
- Never forget how rubbish it was to work for someone else to follow their dream.

As you can see there are many suggestions with good advice, but don't worry if it looks like a lot, perhaps overwhelming, it's simply to make you think. Every person will have a different view and emphasis on what advice they would give to someone new to business.

Bursting the Business Bubble

If you think having a business is right for you and it will be easy you may be in for a surprise. If you're going to be using your existing skill set, do you think by doing exactly the same work but for yourself it will be better and more satisfying?

If you're dissatisfied with where you are going and what you are doing now is it going to change because you've put yourself in charge? You'll have another set of problems to add to the ones you already have.

If you're going to do the same work, change the formula on how you will do it.

- How will you choose what area your business needs to be in?
- Are you going to be targeting another group of people, will the way you provide your services be different? Or,
- Are you looking to find your own niche within a particular area?

Bursting the Bubble

Life changing events have an impact

Perhaps you're wondering how I became a Foot Health Practitioner, after all, it is very different from an office job with the police! It may seem an odd place to start, but let's move back in time to when I was growing up. How you are brought up and nurtured as a child significantly impacts the person you become.

As a little girl, no one in my family had any aspirations for me as to what I could be when I 'grew up' or what job I could do as an adult. In fact, there was no thought I would be particularly interested in or good at anything. All I intrinsically knew was; I didn't want to work in an office as it was, "just sooooo boring." However, I was told, as were many others at the time, in fact, it was drilled into us from a young age, to be a success in life you must have the right qualifications and when you leave school you must get a job no matter what.

There was no encouragement to run a business and I had no aspiration to be a business owner, or do anything different. In fact, Business Studies was only taught at a boys school and my school was all girls. While various ideas flitted in my head, I didn't have a solid base or reassurance to know anything was right or if I was capable of doing it. You may be surprised to learn I have a degree; a joint honours in Fine Art and History of Art, yet when I came to getting a job it wasn't within Art. I was under pressure, "To get a job or I'd be nothing but a failure." Bizarrely, I'd even learnt how to type at school because it was considered a useful skill for a girl to have and it certainly has helped throughout my life. The trouble with being able to type was it moved me straight into office work because this was where most of the jobs were. Art-related work was dismissed because I'd convinced myself I wasn't qualified enough to try. My mindset had been compromised by the culture of the time!

Your mindset and your confidence will affect the choices you make

What I now know and learnt as I grew older is; I am perfectly capable and would have learned what was needed under the right guidance and with the right people helping. This could apply to you as well. Perhaps, qualifications aren't as meaningful as you're lead to believe. The truth is if you end up doing the very thing you didn't want to do then you've got to take charge and do something about it. If you don't like working in an office, like me, but find you are in this situation then you'll understand.

This was my biggest nightmare, but to keep family happy, to have some money and a bit of financial independence this was where I ended up and stayed. After years and years of being slowly ground down and demoralised I'd lost all confidence in myself, my abilities, my self-worth and who I was as a human being and a person. Two major life-changing events in 2007 and 2008 finally made me question where my life was going.

In late September 2007, there was a phone call from Dad, "Your Mum's been rushed to the hospital." We'd only seen her over the weekend, on the Saturday, having been to their house to visit. She'd had some stomach pain and was off her food a bit, but she didn't really complain about it too much. She carried on as normal serving a lovely roast dinner and generally being Mum. You tell yourself it's just 'one of those things', everything is fine and yet now on the Tuesday a few days later she's having emergency surgery.

> ## 126 miles is still 126 miles of worry.

All kinds of thoughts come into your mind, but you try to push them out. There's the worry for a start. I didn't live down the road from Mum and Dad, it was a

126 mile trip from Leicester to Greater London where they lived; 126 miles is still 126 miles of worry.

You're almost counting every single lamp post you pass in the car. Being forced to travel through rush hour traffic, which is never easy at the best of times, further adds to your anxiety when you really want to get somewhere to be with someone you love.

After hours of driving, eventually we arrived and went to Farnborough Hospital (now the Princess Royal Hospital). It was just up the road from my parent's house and was actually the same hospital where I was born. We met Dad who had been told Mum had a blockage which had to be removed and was causing the pain, but there was no further information on Mum's condition. I stayed with Dad and my husband had to go home because of work and his kids who were still living with us. The days merged with Dad and me going to the hospital every day to see Mum who wasn't well, but didn't want to be a nuisance or a bother. There was no information being forwarded as to what was really happening and Dad didn't want to create a fuss either.

I kept telling myself we were going to be told what's up and I was thinking, "It can't be that bad because no one has said anything." Mum was moved to a room on her own and I started to visualise in my mind staying to help Dad to look after her because he'd need some assistance with practicalities. Wednesday and Thursday passed and we were still thinking, "It's going to be OK." Come Friday we had convinced ourselves she'd be coming home.

Someone informed us a member of the palliative care team wanted to speak to us. I didn't know what this word meant or what it entailed; then it was only a word. Sure enough, a middle-aged woman with straight shoulder-length hair arrived holding a clipboard. She wore a hospital lanyard and was *pleasant enough, though she wasn't a nurse. It was about midday and we were sat there expecting news and information about what's going to happen next.*

She led us into a room, supposedly a nicer waiting room for relatives. The room looked like it was last decorated in the 1980s and the walls were painted an apricot colour. It was to make it feel better and more homely, but it didn't. It still felt and smelt like a room you'd expect to see in a hospital. There were cheap prints in flimsy-looking frames on the walls and the practical chairs we had to sit on had a light-coloured wooden frame with horrible dated patterned covers. I was expecting this woman to tell us Mum would be coming home and what we would need to do for her.

"You do know she's not coming home, don't you?" the woman said. Dad didn't do or say anything. He was too shocked. I had to take over.

"How long has she got?"

"A few days if she's lucky. Probably Sunday at the latest or it could be within the next few hours." She's matter of fact giving this information and not unkind.

My world fell away from under my feet. There was no question in my mind of Mum not coming home. She was a cancer survivor; she'd got through it all. "What was this?" "Why?" and "What will happen?" I asked, having never been with someone who'd died. My voice sounded hollow, husky - frightened even.

The woman told us what would happen next. Nature takes over. Mum's breathing would change and gradually slow until it stops; Mum wouldn't be aware of much at the end; and it wouldn't be painful; they were doing all they could to keep her comfortable.

It seemed so unfair as for three whole days no one informed us of Mum's real condition. Didn't they have the decency, courage or respect to tell us the gravity of Mum's situation? It left me wondering why we hadn't pushed for more answers. This restricted behaviour came from taught behaviour; "Don't make a fuss, be polite and someone will come and tell you." It was as my parents had taught me and it was exactly what we did.

Having more information from the start would have given us some time even though it was three short days to prepare, make our peace and properly say our goodbyes to Mum while she could still speak. But there was nothing. The surgeons who had operated on her never came as I was convinced they would and the doctors and nurses we did see and spoke with said nothing. Not a word from any one of them and yet someone must have known the truth, which we were so innocent of. The operation was to ease the pain from the blockage caused by cancer which had been growing undetected in another part of her body. There was no preparation for the devastating news we received from the woman we spoke to. I was utterly convinced Mum was coming home once she'd recovered sufficiently from the operation. And all the time she wasn't.

A few hours later and Mum passed away peacefully, exactly as the woman said it would happen. I was holding her hand with my Dad and brother standing by the bed watching on. You try to say it will be OK, but not knowing if it was or if the right things were said or done.

When it came to making the phone calls to let people know what had happened my Dad couldn't do it and he broke down. It was a massive step out of my comfort zone to make those calls for him and to help organise the funeral because I literally had to take the lead when the way I had been brought up was totally the opposite.

On St George's Day, seven months later, pretty well to the day from Mum's death, I got a phone call *telling me Dad had been rushed to the hospital and I needed to come down immediately. Another 126 miles of worry tackling the busy roads to get to Dad. What was going to happen? What would the outcome be? With the experience of Mum in recent memory I was trying not to think the worst. Arriving at Dad's house, there was still more of a journey to the inner London hospital this time; at the Specialist Heart Unit. More time to worry about what you're going to see and hear.*

I felt like all the responsibility was placed on my shoulders as I spoke to the Specialist in the unit, and I remember his words clearly, "Your father has had a massive insult to his heart."

It can't have been an easy or comfortable conversation for him to start, but I admired his candour and honesty. It made an enormous difference and was the total opposite of what happened with Mum.

He said, "We will do everything we can for him, but he needs to stay sedated so we can treat him because we are doing a lot of tests and procedures and it can be distressing."

My Dad had insisted a phone call was made to me before he went into the ambulance, but I never got to speak to him again. All I could do was sit, watch and wait.

He was on a ward with other people of different ages and when looking at the monitors by their beds they all told a different story. What all the blips and beats and numbers meant and all the lines going up and down on the screens was a mystery.

With reluctance, I had to go home and come back the next day. On return it was the same, lines, numbers, beeps, wires, and tubes. Every now and then I was asked to leave Dad's bedside to go and wait in the waiting room so the nurses could do their work. Saturday turned into Sunday and Sunday turned into

Monday and I am faced with a decision at the end of the day. Do I stay? How do I know what to do for the best? I felt lost and confused.

The relatives room was like a piece of a corridor which had been plucked from nowhere and randomly plonked where it was. At one end there was the door with a clock over it ticking away the hours, the minutes, and the seconds. While at the other end there were two long horizontal and narrow windows placed so high up you couldn't see what was going on outside. All you could see were the grey walls of the corridor and the stark tubular ceiling lights. There was no comfort or interest, looking out of those windows.

Facing each other along the dull walls was a line of utilitarian chairs in a dirty blue colour. As my gaze travelled back into the corner of the room on the left-hand side there was a small round table, with scuffed black metal legs and a scratched faux dark wood varnished top which had a pile of out of date and tatty magazines. The type of titles you'd expect to see in a hospital waiting room. The walls were as grey and as dispirited as I felt. It was a soul-less, airless place to be and with no window to open to let any fresh air in, the warm air smelt stale.

The nurse said, "Well, we'll call you if anything changes." I had to trust there would be enough time to get back, so reluctantly, I left. I knew at home, or to be more accurate, at my parents house, the cat, Cinnamon, needed feeding and looking after so it seemed the best thing to do, to go and wait it out. Arriving back at the house, it was so empty despite all the possessions and memories in it. I was alone waiting to see what the next day would bring because again like before my husband had to go back to our home in Leicester for work and his kids.

In the early hours of the morning, the sound of the telephone ringing woke me and the memory of that *ring tone haunts me to this day. Half asleep I made it downstairs and picked up the phone. It was the sister of the ward. She introduced herself but sounded curt, tense and there was a tightness to her voice. "You need to come to the hospital now!" she said.*

OK, but I didn't know how to get to the hospital and public transport would be too slow at this time of day. Straight away after a short conversation with the sister and the call was ended so I could ring Auntie, my Dad's sister. She lived 7 miles away, which was around 15 minutes away by car. It was dark outside and it all felt very surreal, very quiet. No one else was awake yet.

Like me, Auntie had to get herself up and dressed as well as get her husband ready. He had dementia. She then had to get herself to the house so she could take us all to the hospital. Trying to get dressed and prepared for Auntie to arrive and convincing myself I'd be there in time wasn't easy. The house was cold, gloomy, and lonely in the dark. Not a sound could be heard. There was this horrible apprehension, worry, and uncertainty.

Less than half an hour after putting the phone down the silence was broken with that ring tone. It was another call from the ward sister. "You're too late."

> **You pretend everything's OK**
>
> **when it's anything but OK.**

A short almost brusque conversation followed, but it felt like there was a judgement on me because we didn't make it in time and hadn't tried hard enough to make it to be by Dad's bedside when he passed. Another call to Auntie to say there's no need to rush anymore, but she still came to the house. It was a sorry drive to the hospital driving on nearly deserted streets with the eerie glow of the lamp posts and the bright headlights of passing vehicles.

In the cubicle at the hospital, all the grey tubes and wires and the bits of tape previously attached to Dad were discarded in the bin and the monitor by the bed was quiet and still. I looked in the bin at those bits and pieces with him lying there so still, eyes closed, sleeping, but not sleeping anymore. I felt such a deep regret. It felt so sad and the sadness was worse because I wasn't there for him and should have been there and I'd let him down. I truly believed this although part of me knew he wouldn't have wanted us there at the final moment. You never know when the time will be. It was his time, but I wasn't there to see him through it and hold his hand and say it will be OK.

Again it was me doing the bulk of the work to prepare for the funeral along with Auntie's help. Making the round of phone calls again was so much harder this time because it was so soon after Mum's passing. To get those words out or to utter the sounds of those terrible words, "Dad has gone" was so painful. You pretend everything's OK when it's anything but OK.

Families can be your biggest help. Or they can be your biggest hindrance.

Do you want your life to change?

The events of 2007 and 2008 brought with them the realisation, my life needed to change because life is taken so quickly. Like anyone else both my parents were living their lives.

Going through their personal effects there were the new shoes, a handbag and clothes which Mum had bought a couple of weeks before and never got to wear or use.

> ## Going through someone else's life reminds you of the fragility of your own.

My Dad on the other hand created a little wish list of things he wanted to do and particular things he wanted to buy. I guess it was all the things Mum had said, "You can't have that, or what do you want that for?" It was like he was free and could go out and get all these things without anyone saying no.

Going through someone else's life reminds you of the fragility of your own. I was unhappy with my life and at 35 years old was no longer somebody's child. Every Mother's Day and Father's day I am reminded of this fact and have no children of my own to soften the blow.

I was deeply unhappy at work and when walking into the office each day and being ignored, after saying, "Good morning," made it very depressing. Sitting at a desk in a room with most of the lights off because people didn't like the glare on their screens and looking out the window to a lifeless red brick wall was no fun either. Each day the same. Staring at my screen trying to keep myself together, stay alert, and concentrate on my work was very difficult. The office environment was making me sick physically and mentally.

Looking back, part of me wonders how I put up with it for so long. I realise now it is better to be stronger and make every day count than to live an unfulfilled life. Today, when having a bad day running my own business I'm in a better place than I was then. It takes time to heal mentally and spiritually, but you have to stop looking back and living in the past and move forward.

What happened is the work situation and the personal grief made me realise my life needed to change especially because of the impact on my health, well-being and personal relationships. It also made me realise; I could be more in control of my destiny and life but allowing other people to dictate and control it wasn't working.

> It was an enormous shock to lose both my parents so suddenly and the shock was made bigger when I noticed others were carrying on as normal and had no idea what was coming. I didn't want my life to end in a chapter of it where I was living a life I hated, which was also destroying me physically and mentally. If I hadn't left the hated job when I did, I would have ended up in a coffin.

- What is your life like right now?
- Is the situation you are in currently making you want to start a business?

Meanwhile, you'll find out in the next chapter how feet and foot health came into the picture in mine.

2: Enlightened People Are Attracted To The Right Business

You've decided having a business is right for you. It's going to be a new start and you want to use this to move forward in your life. You will either be transitioning from what you do now to become more independent, using existing skill sets and what you've learned over the years to create a business or you may decide to pursue something totally different.

What attracts you to the profession or business you intend to pursue? Are there similar businesses in your area or chosen niche? How established and successful are they? What will the competition be like? Will there be enough custom? Are you going to be taking over an existing business? You'll need to do some research to make sure whatever you choose you are making the right choice.

Find out if what you want to do is feasible and if you'll need some new qualifications. Don't delude yourself into believing cheap courses are going to make you an expert. You have to be realistic and practical about this particularly if it's a professional qualification you're pursuing. You'll need continued support and if you have no real guidance on maintaining your professional development this can also put your chosen area or industry into disrepute. Consider if the cost in time and money invested in learning new skills is going to be worth it in the long term.

Open your mind to business

It's your business. Your choices. You may or may not believe it is important to carry on with your personal or your Continuing Professional Development (CPD). Some people genuinely think when they leave school, that's it. They've had all the education they need and don't need to further themselves anymore. Do you think this way? Are you the person who when you are offered opportunities to do some new learning or training you don't want to know and you're not interested in it? You need to be honest with yourself here. If you have this mindset, are you going to be the right person to start your own business?

A big contributory factor of businesses which don't last, survive or succeed is they don't change or move forward when there are problems or adversities they have to face. They've never taken advice, learning, or development and have continued to make the same mistakes over and over.

> **There is always something new you can learn.**

Having your own business is a lot about continuous professional and or personal development. The people who do the best are continuously developing and expanding their knowledge base and skill sets in all areas of their life. They don't assume they know it all; there is always something new you can learn. You need to have an open and enquiring mind. In fact if you don't take any learning, you may become the barrier for your business to grow.

Many people who start their own businesses aren't suitable for it and don't have the right personality. Consider taking a personality profile – it can give great understanding into your character - why you think as you do and how you interact with others. There are many different tests to choose from and can be completed online. They are very insightful and if you can understand your strengths and weaknesses this can help you to focus on your most positive skill sets to get the most out of yourself and others as well. Two tests with different approaches I have tried and found to be very insightful were DISC profiling and Clifton Strengths.

Sometimes the person who you think would be least successful at running a business turns out to be very good at it because they already had the aptitude to do it. Those attitudes and resilience were already there, but never got teased out in the right way in what they were doing previously. It happens to a lot of people. If your talents and strengths go unrecognised you'll stagnate where you are.

Steps to becoming a Foot Health Practitioner

There came a point where I couldn't even think clearly at work and when an opportunity was given for the redundancy process it was too much to even contemplate taking because I didn't want to let anyone down. Redundancy can be a bad experience if you let it. Lack of confidence in yourself and your skills can stop you from making the right decisions.

After losing both my parents' there was so much to do. The sale of their house, dealing with the solicitor, estate agent, personal issues, my family life including selling our own home and buying another, which needed to be extended and renovated before we could move in. At the end of it all, a small sum of money was left over. Rather than waste it, I decided to do something different and because I desperately wanted to leave the job, the idea of starting a business occurred. The thought was so appealing because it was the fantasy of being your own boss and being independent with no one to answer to.

Your mind goes through different ideas of what you'd like to do. Very randomly feet, yes feet came to my mind. It had been dabbled with a few years before through my good friend, Dorothy, who had been very supportive after the death of my parents'. Dear Dorothy, was also my spiritual mother and told me she was seeing a chiropodist. Being intrigued about what a chiropodist does I asked to tag along. At Dorothy's appointment, this very grumpy rude woman sullenly answered my questions whilst doing Dorothy's feet. It's not the best selling point for a potential career, but it was interesting, and looking at what this grumpy rude woman was doing knew straight away I could do way better.

> **You should always know yourself**
>
> **and what your limits are.**

Years later in 2010, and remembering the encounter, I went online looking for something similar and found a course in Birmingham at The College of Foot Health Practitioners for something called a Foot Health Practitioner (FHP). Previous dalliances into doing podiatry convinced me it is a seriously long degree and really hard work with a lot of information to absorb and learn. Knowing my own mental health and personal situation at the time, I knew it wasn't going to be practical. You should always know yourself and what your limits are.

To be a Foot Health Practitioner you are required to do Continuing Professional Development to maintain the qualification as it's monitored by a Professional Standards Authority, which made it more appealing. Maybe, just maybe, it could bring some independence, self-respect, and something better back into my life. Work-life was unhappy and the job security wasn't there.

I remember going to the college and upon arriving was introduced to Victor Fletcher (now retired), who was a typical Brummie man - short and stout with a proud heart. He showed me around, talking about the place and the course, how he and John Falkner-

Heylings, his business partner, had started the college. The building itself was a rabbit warren with rooms, corridors, and doorways going here and there, up and down steps and narrow stairways and passageways. (Fortunately, the college has now moved to more modern premises). In the treatment rooms, there were students diligently attending to people and their feet; what they were doing looked possible for me to do. It didn't seem so hard or out of reach to learn what they were doing. The small sum of money left after all the renovations to the house was exactly the right amount to pay for the course.

Rabbit Warren

In between the job I hated while pretending everything was OK, the course work was completed and passed. Once done it was off to the college for a couple of weeks to do the final practical assessments and some classroom teaching. It took a year to complete the course in total and I qualified as a Foot Health Practitioner in December 2011 and the business started in March 2012. It was really exciting because this was the golden ticket out of the hated job and would be the proverbial two fingers to it. This was the change which was going to empower me and give back something lost in myself after years of leading a life I hated.

Those years had been a difficult time for me mentally, emotionally, and spiritually. The loss of someone close to you creates changes and challenges in your life particularly if they have been a significant and constant part of it. The grounded feeling knowing Mum and Dad were there even if it was at the end of a phone was gone, while the loss of them both so unexpectedly and suddenly wasn't an easy transition to overcome either.

Alongside everything else which was going on, there was also my own very severe depression. My husband doesn't remember what I had to deal with especially as he didn't understand depression so found it hard to support me. It wasn't easy for any of us and he remembers me being difficult, without realising there was a lot of hard to deal with issues' not only at home, but at work too.

At work, I was always the problem person and every day was suffering mentally in one way or another. No matter what was said or done it got misconstrued. The only person who could offer any kindness and consolation was my friend, dear Dorothy. When it got really bad at work, she would get a phone call, which was unbelievably often.

I ended up on long-term sick due to the bullying and stress. You might have thought the house was haunted because I was like a ghost, sleeping hours on end, waking up in the dead of night, and restlessly wandering around the house without making a sound in the darkness. You would have seen a soulless, lifeless, and pale figure reflected in the glass of the windows while all around everyone else slept.

Dorothy told me, "You shouldn't go back to work, you're not well enough," when she was told after 6 months on the sick I had to go back. She was right, but the doctors were pressing me to go back to work because they said the interaction with people makes you feel better. My husband wanted me to go back because of the financial situation we were in with credit cards full and bills to pay.

There was so much pressure to return to work, but it was like exchanging one living nightmare for another. When finally returning to work from being on long-term sick it was from full-time hours to part-time. The working conditions and the people had made me so ill it was impossible to work full time anymore.

The stress, the bullying, the isolation, and all I had endured took their toll not only physically and mentally, but now financially. Initially, it was a three-day week, but even this was too much as it was so exhausting. Time at work dragged and there was the constant stress and worry about going back after rest days which didn't help either.

> **You tell yourself a disproportionate number of untruths and harbour negative thoughts.**

GET OUT OF JAIL FREE

Get out of Jail Card

Upheavals at work resulted in constant restructuring and departmental changes, each one brought threatened redundancies. When the opportunity was offered for redundancy at work, I didn't have the courage to take it and strongly believe if I had it would have created a greater will, impetus, and focus to get the business working better sooner. Fear is a terrible emotion. You tell yourself a disproportionate number of untruths and harbour negative thoughts which aren't true and listen to the little voice in your head instead of looking at and analysing the facts.

I ended up on a team with some different people. The introduction to my new team wasn't the best because they were told I had been a problem in the other office where I worked. At least the people got to know me as a person and realised underneath there was actually a human being. Some of us still keep in touch today which I am grateful for.

The get out of jail free card

Becoming qualified as an FHP meant so much more than gaining a certificate for passing and completing a course. It represented the move towards freedom and self-worth. Suddenly you go from being A.N. Employee, used to the regular pay, the sick pay, the security, and everything else which goes with it to becoming a Business Owner.

Back then the concept of running a business was incomprehensible to me, a whole new different world. When starting the business my mindset was in an unhealthy place, I didn't even feel entitled to receive good feedback or go places to meet other business people. I thought I'd be laughed at because of what I didn't know and because the clinic didn't have much custom. A whole load of opportunities, advice, learning, friendships, relationships, and nurturing was missed.

23

However, the business was started from scratch with next to no help. It's making a difference to so many people. When you start your business, you'll tell yourself "It's mine," which is so liberating because it really is such an achievement to start a business and to keep it going.

The business was deliberately started part-time because of wanting the security blanket of having the job and the regular pay. Every single day dragged and every minute was an agony and it made sense to move the job down from a 3-day week to a 2-day week to give a break between the business and the job. Looking back there was this constant stress about going back into the office. Those two days were too much, but still, there wasn't the inner confidence to really step back and leave once and for all.

There was a 'get out of jail free' card and this was the business. It was so empowering to know it was there. The business meant everything. Having more knowledge about business would have helped, but new customers were coming to the clinic and slowly the business began to grow.

My husband wasn't keen on me leaving the job, although he wouldn't have stopped me. If you have a partner or spouse who is not ready themselves to have you leave your job it will make it even harder to take this step.

The fear of losing a reliable income and moving into unknown territory is very real and very strong. If you do background research and consider the suggestions in this book it will help you make the decision from a stronger position and mindset. By making the best choices for yourself and your business you'll only move forward.

3: A Curious Person Starts With Questions

As part of the planning process, there are lots of questions and details you should consider and think about.

- How will you finance your business?
- What kind of space do you need and where will you be located?
- Are you going to be travelling to people or are they going to be coming to you?
- What do you actually need to do what you do?
- Do you need a qualification?
- What kinds of products and services will you be providing?
- How much is all the equipment, tools and applications you need for your business going to cost?
- How much will it cost to run your business?
- What do you need to have in place to make the experience the best it can be for the people you deal with?
- What would meet their expectations?
- How are you going to safeguard your own future?

To carry on working in the 'Day Job' or not

Financial concerns are always going to be at the heart of any business.

- Do you have enough resilience to start a business?

With no savings and unable to leave your job you will have to carry on working because you need the money for the mortgage or rent, your bills and living costs, etc. In this case can you use the evening and weekends to start growing your business?

> **Shut yourself off from the wrong energies and find the best people who can help you.**

If you're still in a job and working with people sharing negative mindsets or attitudes, it's going to affect you. What people say and do may be well-intentioned, it could be banter, but if it's not helping you mentally, you'll have to learn to ignore it and remind yourself why you're going to start or have started your business.

- Do you have a defined timescale in mind?

This is where having a plan can help. Don't become too comfortable where you are now, or you'll be less likely to take action. Remember to shut yourself off from the wrong energies and find the best people who can help you, encourage and support you in the right way.

More Questions

- Can you separate your business from work by reducing your hours?
- If you haven't got the resilience to reduce your hours or to build your business outside of work, can you save money?
- Are you disciplined and resolved enough to build up some savings without allowing other temptations to use them?

Setting a specific sum to start your business with could become the excuse to not start your business. Don't stop yourself from moving forward because you haven't achieved the exact amount you wanted to have saved up.

Savvy people could even look at attracting investors for their business and it could be someone such as a relative or friends. Again, if you do this protect your own and their interests by agreeing a contract so there is no recompense down the line. Take sound advice from someone with proper knowledge and experience in this area. You hear stories about friends or family lending money to someone they know for a business venture and when the relationship has gone sour they can't get their money back. Money can be a very emotive subject. Using a professional investor with whom you have no emotional ties may work better.

With my start-up I was still working part-time alongside the business with my husband's salary there for support.

Consider the impact of financials on your situation especially if your other half or family need to be supported by what you're doing or if they are going to be supporting you financially. They will need to know and understand what the impact will be and how it will affect them.

Location and ambience are key

Having the right location for your business is key. Let's say you plan to run your business at your home address.

To start, my clinic room was upstairs, but I had to change the layout for easier access for my clients. By putting a wall in, I created a new downstairs clinic room. This was much more practical particularly for people who didn't like going up and down the stairs due to mobility issues.

When you have a business in your home, it's not only about your own practicalities, but also for clients you will be inviting in. It helps if you can situate your working areas somewhere separate so there is less traffic going though living spaces.

If someone comes to your business no matter where it is located, you've got to think about what they want when they come to see you. If you're offering some sort of service and it feels like your attention is less than one hundred percent on them, then any distractions no matter how small can deflect from them having the value and enjoyment they deserve.

If you work alone, you may find some background noise or music stimulating and comforting. Certainly, if your service means you wish to introduce some music or calming sounds be sensitive to the needs of the people you serve. It's their experience so be respectful. I focus on a noise and it stops me from zoning out and relaxing. Never assume to know what people want or how they will experience your product or service. Ask them! For instance: Are you happy, comfortable or satisfied?

Space to Work

If you are looking to run your business from your home, think on these questions:

- What is the layout and how is the setup?
- Can you have the room you'll be using as near as possible to the front door?
- How can you avoid traffic going through your physical home and personal spaces?

There's no use in telling yourself you'll keep overheads down by running your business from your home if the space and environment you have available aren't appropriate.

You've got to have a dedicated space where you can work as a professional.

- Is the room you're intending to use the most creative or best space for you to be working in?
- How are you going to separate your work from your home life?
- How will your working space impact on other family members?
- How professional will it look to people?
- Is it an appropriate space for what you are doing?

You'll need to create a space and defined area where you can work in the home with minimal distractions so you can work more effectively and efficiently. Don't forget to check if working from home will affect other household payments such as your mortgage, rent and business rates. Weigh up the pros and cons of working at home to help make your decision.

If working from home is not practical or viable then you will need to consider having a business premises. You'll want the best location possible. Ask yourself:

- Can people easily find you?
- Is there adequate parking?
- What other businesses are in the area?
- Will these impact on your business?
- If you need peace and quiet, are there businesses nearby which create lots of noise?

- Consider what the best way forward is for you. You need to think about how long term each set of circumstances is going to be and how much it will cost.
- What is the most financially viable way of working?

You can find office spaces and rooms to hire for the hour or day so you don't have to pay for a permanent office. With short-term spaces, an additional bonus could include other facilities there such as a reception, additional security, cleaners, etc. A lot of people lease premises.

- What happens when the business has got more revenue?
- Will you need to move to larger premises or a better location?

If you're going to lease a property, obviously there will be a cost. Remember, whatever your long-term strategy is, whether you lease or own it with property there will be maintenance and repairs either way. When you lease you still have to pay to make the space fit your needs and have it fitted out. Make sure you understand what you are responsible for paying.

There's no point in having the perfect location if through the services you provide you aren't able to cover your basic costs and in the worst-case scenario are running at a loss.

Investing in equipment

Investing in the right equipment is rather like finding a good pair of shoes. It will make what you do so much easier, and a good investment will last.

- Can you afford to have the equipment you need?
- Some items can be really expensive, even if you have paid for them outright.
- Will you need to pay service fees to keep it compliant?
- Remember ownership isn't the end of the costs for equipment. You are also responsible for the upkeep and maintenance of it.

- How much longevity has the equipment got and will the value of it depreciate?

In certain businesses equipment quickly becomes obsolete. Would you need to regularly replace and update it to keep up with your competition? Think about quality too because your business is as much about how you are portrayed or perceived.

- Does it fit your business model to be presented in a certain way?

Sometimes it may be more economical for you to hire furniture and equipment because if it doesn't work out, you can finish the hire agreement or upgrade, and in time move on. In some industries, it's actually quite normal to do this, but it's also a good way to test what suits you and your business. Industry-specific equipment can be expensive so it may actually give you a better option than if you were to try to buy it yourself. If you can source it, you could try good quality reconditioned furniture and equipment to use.

Always consider the most practical and financially viable solution first in every situation. Remember, when you hire equipment to account for costs related to it in your monthly outgoings. It is essential to check the small print to make sure you understand what is and isn't included within any agreement. If you're going to be using a vehicle regularly and running up the mileage on it would it be better to lease a vehicle, which can be regularly changed or upgraded?

Look at everything you'll use or be doing for your business in detail from the car you need to use to visit clients, attend meetings, to your business rates (if applicable), electricity costs, rent, furnishings, equipment, entertaining clients, lighting, general upkeep, and maintenance, etc.

Once you know exactly what you need, where you will be situated or working from, you can work out what it is all going to cost. Conducting a proper costing exercise will give you the true cost of what you're planning to do with your business, and it may surprise you how much it will be.

Are you charging enough?

It's easy to assume if one business is charging a certain amount, and another is charging a different amount then if you charge the lower amount, you'll make a living and attract more customers, but it doesn't work like this. You see people trying to copy what other businesses are doing then wonder why they struggle to earn a living. Undercutting your prices against other businesses doesn't necessarily give you a better type of customer or more customers or even more profit.

> **Whatever you do, make sure what you charge is cost-effective.**

Charging less to attract more customers is likely to bring you the person who wants to pay less but wants more from you. They're unlikely to try other services you may have on offer because they only care about price and not value.

Whatever you do, make sure your charges are cost-effective. Your aim should be to run and have a viable business giving you a good income and the life you deserve. It's not only about generating extra income, but offering more value to the people visiting your business and about them spending as much of their time and money with you.

- Will you be selling other products?
- Is it going to be something added to the service you provide which costs a bit extra?

If you have a limited product or service there is less room to make more money from the people you serve and if you've not really thought about the bigger packages, services, and deals, which you can offer and create then now is the time to do so. Even if you offer a limited range to start you can expand and introduce new products and services as your business grows.

You could learn by visiting another business, as research, to see what they do, to see if you can pick up any ideas to adapt and transfer into your own business. It gives you an idea of what the competition is doing, what services, offers and products they have and what they are charging. It's not about copying because you want your business model, product, and services to be unique to you and your business. It can give you an idea of how to base your prices, but remember to focus on your business, what is right for it, and the people you will ultimately be dealing with.

Know the value of what you offer

People will have their own perceptions as to what they should receive from the products or service(s) you give.

There was an enlightening article detailing what happened when a woman complained about the service she received at a little cafe. It was a small independent business and she'd gone in there to meet with some friends and didn't want to buy anything. She asked for a glass of hot water with a slice of lemon and expected this should be given to her for free. When she got charged for it, she complained and gave the business a bad review.

The response of the business owner was clear, honest, and insightful because it was answered in terms of what it actually cost for this woman to have a glass of hot water with a slice of lemon in their cafe. It wasn't only the cost of paying the person who made and served her the drink, the cost of electricity to light the premises, and run other appliances, etc. It was also the time she was sat at the table meaning another paying customer could not sit there and a whole long list of other areas contributing to the day-to-day running costs of the business. It was a very detailed answer, but it made a really potent point.

People don't always appreciate the true cost of running a business and what you have to pay out simply to have them in the room. So many aspects will affect your overheads and costs. You need to sit down, record and consider carefully every expenditure you will need to make. It's very easy when you start a business to spend lots of money, but not knowing exactly where all the money is going either because you aren't keeping track of the details. It's easy to lose track of little costs occurring in the background. Remember, the cost insurance and similar necessary items usually increase each year.

Take good, sound financial advice

Find someone with experience such as a mentor to go over the figures. Get it right because your costs will affect what your prices will be. Get it wrong and you'll be running at a loss.

> **Good financial advice and planning**
>
> **is like investing in good shoes.**

You want your business to be making you money. Good financial advice and planning is like investing in good shoes and like a good pair of shoes this will give you the right protection. Hopefully, the money the business is going to make will see you through the good and bad times, but any amount of money is irrelevant if you haven't managed or invested it wisely.

When you have a flow of money for your business put portions aside in different 'pots' or accounts to cover insurances, marketing, courses, upkeep, etc. Remember to include your own personal income. You still need to plan for your future because it's very easy when you think you have lots of money coming in to spend it.

A prime example of this is a friend of mine whose friend was selling products through a company with her husband and they were really successful. They were having lots of holidays each year and were like the 'Golden Couple' in the company because of their success and all was going really well. Then they were falsely reported for something they hadn't done and the company removed them.

All they had built up and worked for over the years, the business income, the bonuses, and everything alongside it was taken away.

To make the situation even worse they had an endowment mortgage (where you pay the interest) on their beautiful forever home, and had assumed a sizeable cash lump would arrive at the end to pay whatever was left. This didn't happen and they didn't have the means to pay any deficit. All those wonderful holidays, the big beautiful house, the fabulous lifestyle meant nothing when they were faced with losing all of it because they didn't carefully save and seriously plan for their future.

Seek expert financial advice

Take good financial advice from an expert to make sure everything which matters to you the most (not only your business) are properly protected, and insured, to make sufficient provisions for your future including illness insurance. As an established employee in a workplace you still expect to be paid if you fall sick with money to cover your living expenses while you are off work.

> **Have at least 6 month's worth of money (reserves) put to one side.**

- What would happen to you, your business, and your home life if you fell ill?
- What happens with the money you provide for yourself for your own personal expenses?
- If anything were to happen are your personal interests and revenue protected?

It is suggested you should have at least 6-month's worth of money (reserves) put to one side to cover your business and personal expenses at all times. Take action now before the unthinkable happens because you hear stories of business owners falling ill with no money, not only to cover their business, but their personal expenses too.

Do you need to make a Will? Nobody falls ill intentionally, and you don't want your business to fail because you weren't well enough to keep it running. Of course, the worst-case scenario would be if you passed away. Having a living Will protects the interests not only of your loved ones, but will ensure your wishes are attended to should the very worst happen.

Starting out, provision should be made to cover the business for at least the first 6 months. When those savings are gone you should be managing with the revenue from the business and hopefully starting to build those savings up again, but what happens if the business stops?

My friend's husband was subjected to a horrific assault, which left him unable to work for a significant length of time. While he recovered there was no money and they had to survive on their savings. Ready or not when the money ran out, he had to go back to work. It's a worrying and stressful situation to be in.

Other points outside of your control can take away your business income. e.g. Lockdown due to Covid-19 started in 2020, and this is what happened to me.

I was caught out; having signed up for a course as the next step in my speaker journey. So long as I was training everything would work out revenue wise. Covid-19 happened, and courses had to be cancelled. Other unforeseen expenditures occurred meaning the timing couldn't have been worse. Bills were coming from different directions.

Fortunately, there were some savings and my husband's job still brought some income albeit in a diminished form because he could no longer do overtime. Taking the correct steps for the business to move it forward as well as to raise my profile came to naught when the income suddenly disappeared. Anything could have happened. My husband could have been made redundant, his hours could have been cut at work or I could have been too ill to work. For you, it could be similar or the care of an elderly relative, your child, etc. There are so many aspects of life over which you have absolutely no control.

If you have little money and you've lost a significant amount of income, as with the Covid-19 situation, then how are you going to manage? Many practitioners (in my industry) were saying how they had to go and find jobs to bring money in, while others had to sign up for state benefit to manage. Not everybody received money from the government nor expected this either.

Business Structure

Are you going to be a sole trader or self-employed if it is only yourself?

Being a sole trader is all about your business structure, while if you are self-employed, it simply means you're not employed by anyone else or you pay tax through PAYE. You can still be a self-employed sole trader if you run your business by yourself and you could have a limited company, but still be self-employed.

Whatever you are, you will need to register your business with the HMRC within 3 months of setting up and you'll be responsible for your self-assessment tax return each year and you pay the relevant tax on the profit you make.

Don't forget as well to make sure you keep up with your National Insurance contributions. This can all be done through your accountant and a financial advisor would guide you through what is best for you and your business. When you leave your job and have your own business, you're responsible for making sure your contributions continue.

If you become a limited company, you need to register with Companies House, but this could be an action you take later on as the business grows.

It's not only about what's happening with your business today, but also in the future:

- What happens when you retire from your business?
- What is your plan?
- Are you going to sell your business when you retire?

Just because your business makes money doesn't mean it is saleable. If the business relies on you to make it work, you may become unstuck. Put it this way, if you weren't in the equation, could your business run without you?

Know your processes

Systems and procedures are good for any business and define how you deal with different events and scenarios in your business, they also add continuity and flow. As your business grows you will have more systems and procedures as you encounter them and grow in experience.

Every single part of the process matters and should be recorded on how it is done including how you do specific tasks. Keeping a record of processes is particularly pertinent if you intend to expand and have other people working for you in your business and also ultimately to sell it if this is your intention.

When I started my business, I followed some rough guidance from the college and put adverts in local magazines. A friend of mine, Jane, wanted to be the very first customer, which was very exciting. Jose, a lady who used to give me reflexology treatments also booked an appointment. It was also a way to give me feedback on what I was doing. If you do this it will give you the chance to test what you are doing on people you are familiar with.

How will you take orders and make appointments?

- If it is a phone call, do you have an answering machine to take messages?
- Are people going to be contacting you online? How are you recording this? When people contact you how are you following up?
- Is it automated to save time?
- Are you going to keep a record of where you are receiving your leads from?

Measure and record the details and you will be able to take action to reach the right people.

- Will you need terms and conditions or a contract?

There are standard templates you can copy, but you may want to have them checked over by a professional. Membership of your local Chamber of Commerce means you will gain access to useful materials, templates and documents which you can customise.

Don't forget data protection and GDPR are key these days. Be aware of the rules surrounding these areas and how they apply to your business.

- Where will you store information about your clients?
- How will you protect the information you hold on people?
- What information exactly will you be taking from them?
- Is the information you hold on people relevant?
- How will you be taking payment?
- How will you weed files in the future? Weeding files is the process of going through your paperwork and electronic files and sifting through what is relevant and pertinent to keep. There are rules under GDPR on keeping personal information on people. Make sure you are aware of

current best practice and legislation. Dispose of data correctly. You may need a shredder.

The less friction there is for taking payment the easier it will be for people to pay you. Contactless payment and ways to pay online means cash flows so much quicker. You have to keep up with this. The more ways you can arrange for people to pay you which are convenient to them the more likely it is they will want to use you and your services.

One of the best decisions I took for my business was to have a card machine which has costs, but having a card machine means people spend more money making the cost worth it.

What you would have seen at the beginning of my business is me running my clinic from home, but still going to work and there was a duality of working. You may find once you start your business you have more confidence, not only in yourself, but in your abilities as you're discovering a defined value from what you're doing.

On the other hand, if you're still working you may find your job negatively affects you and it can be for different reasons from the job itself to the people you are working or dealing with.

With my business, it was so satisfying to hear someone say after one appointment at the clinic their feet actually felt and looked so much better. It is incredibly powerful and liberating even now to receive positive feedback.

I'm sure you would want to have a business giving you satisfaction, even if it's solely to hear someone say they're very pleased with the work you've done for them.

For me it wasn't a happy situation at my existing work. There were still instances where the team faced redundancy, again, I didn't embrace redundancy when they were offered. It was a big mistake because what happened during the first years in the business, was there was the comfort blanket of the job as A.N. Employee receiving regular pay and then treating myself as A.N. Employee in my own business, without thinking or behaving as a business owner should.

Eventually, you realise there needs to be a change as you may start to notice comments in your email or on your social media due to the way you've been browsing and watching others online. For me it was a desire to change the way I thought from a poor mindset to a more fluid mind-flow. Mindset suggests something which is immobile and fixed, while mind-flow has movement and change at its core. I recognised the existing mindset and mental health were really poor and needed addressing. Working in an office with a load of negative energies didn't help either.

Don't be in a race to the bottom

For the first four years of my business prices weren't raised due to a lack of confidence. This may astonish you but some people don't increase their prices because of the fear of losing existing custom! However, there wouldn't be a viable business if you carried on in this way.

You've got to grow your business and it's not only about having more custom, you need to factor in increasing costs. Your utility bills increase, the cost to run your vehicle goes up, insurance goes up and so it goes on, therefore why would you feel bad to increase your own prices? There are always going to be the people who don't want to pay the extra. They'll gripe over the smallest amounts of money.

Maybe you can relate to this. I've heard other practitioners talk about how the very modest prices they charge are quibbled by the people they go to see. These businesses receive no help from the local authorities, NHS or anywhere else because they are a private practice. What on earth do these people think?

When you try explain your costs, professional knowledge, and an increase in those all have a value, etc you're treated dismissively. Unfortunately, many practitioners will be familiar with the scene. The person they are dealing with may have a large, detached bungalow, the furniture in their home, is of good quality albeit a bit dated, but well looked after. Maybe a gardener or relative is attending to the very large immaculate garden and you can hear the sound of a sit on mower, which is housed within a huge outbuilding when not in use. Perhaps those very same people will have hairdressers visit, people to do manicures, the meals they have delivered are of an expensive brand and they often talk about taking the family out for treats. Some practitioners relate how the people who complain about cost will then disclose giving large amounts of money to grandchildren to spend on holidays, but still ask for the pensioner rate. If you try to increase your prices, they'll tell you someone else charged less, but they're no longer practicing, or they'd have gone to them. It is so disheartening.

They will say everything they can to make you feel guilty for charging what you are worth. A lot of practitioners cave in because they feel guilty about charging in the first place.

I never felt guilty about increasing prices, it was the fear of losing the customers I had. There was never a mass exodus of people leaving the business and over time the clinic acquired better customers who were willing to pay for their healthcare. When I had someone challenge me, I felt angry. I worked hard for my qualification and was really insulted especially as it was obvious, they could afford it.

> **Cheap labour isn't skilled.**
>
> **Skilled labour isn't cheap.**

Sometimes it's as much about developing and listening to your customers and changing to meet their needs, wants, and requirements. In business, you've got to focus on the people who want to move with you and your business. The people who refuse to pay a little bit extra each year really are not your ideal customer or client. Yes, to start with when price increases were introduced there were some gentle protestations from some, but now people know what to expect because they know the service they receive and are happy to accept it.

I was intrigued by these dilemmas so put this question in a group of entrepreneurs on social media:

How do you deal with the customers who want you to lower your prices because other people charge less? The responses were brilliant and really helped to give a perspective.

- You can't put a price on quality. If you lower your price you will devalue your service and products. It also devalues you psychologically. It's about profit, not pennies. Sell your quality and service, which justify a price.
- If you lower your prices, you're proving your worth.
- Don't be desperate in hard times. Don't be in a race to the bottom.
- Let the person offering the cheaper price provide the service then you can charge double your price. (Not everyone agreed you should charge more). Once people learn their mistake, they will come back to you.
- Your price is your price and when people realise you are the best they can find locally they will be happy they have found you and will come back time and time again.
- Cheap labour isn't skilled. Skilled labour isn't cheap.
- Some people are so much about price over quality so their service seems like a scam.
- Encourage your customers to ask searching questions to the same company offering the same for less. People often think they are receiving the same (like for like) when they aren't.
- If someone wants to start chipping away at the price it can be a warning sign; they aren't going to be a good customer.

Race to the Bottom

- Attract different customers. Understand your value. Customers who can't afford your services will drain your resources and cost you money and further opportunities.

Not everybody will want to pay less. In fact, someone said in her business it was the poorer people who valued her more and would never complain about or quibble the price.

There will also be people who for whatever reason and you don't always know why, stop using your services. It might feel like the end of a relationship and hopefully, you're welcoming in new people in their wake. Circumstances in anyone's life such as their own health issues, the health issues of a family member could take their time and energy as well as other reasons.

One lady suddenly stopped coming to the clinic then five years later out of the blue sent an email wanting an appointment. Personal issues in her life meant she hadn't been able to come and now the time was right for her to return.

Whatever is happening overall in your business there should always be growth and progression. If you serve and look after the people who matter the best you can, gain new custom, and you will maintain and grow a healthy business with reliable customers.

Your plan is not only what you intend to do, but should also encompass your core values and the vision or big idea for your business.

4: Smart People Have A Successful Plan

Every good business should have some sort of plan and structure to follow. I didn't have a solid plan to start. Some say it doesn't matter so much, while others advocate writing a plan. The point is if you have no idea of what you are doing, where you are going, and how you are going to achieve your goals in your business then how will you monitor and measure your progress and achievements? If your growth is slow, you have no goals without any intention to remedy it you wont be prepared when circumstances change. In the same way, if your growth is faster than expected without a plan you will struggle.

Steps towards the perfect plan

How do you write a business plan which is realistic and has achievable and viable goals? A lot of people become confused because they don't know how to make a realistic plan on how to grow a business. Your plan is not only what you intend to do, what kind of income streams your business will have, but should also encompass your core values and the vision or big idea for your business. Knowing your core values and vision will help you to define what your business is about and who and what kind of people it is there to serve.

Any goal or plan needs a structure. The most commonly known and shared is the **SMART** system originally devised by George T Doran whose definition tied in five criteria:

Plan for Success

- **S**pecific: Target a specific area for improvement.
- **M**easurable: Quantify, or at least suggest, an indicator of progress.
- **A**ssignable: Specify who will do it.
- **R**ealistic: State what results can realistically be achieved given available resources.
- **T**ime-related: Specify when the result can be achieved.

Some people include 2 extra steps on SMART goals to create **SMARTER** goals - a 7 step system. Thus

- **E**valuate: Assess your goals daily.
- **R**eadjust: Change your methods and techniques if what you are doing isn't working.

The importance of evaluating your goals means you are more likely to achieve them because you are less likely to ignore them. If what you are doing is not working readjusting your goals will help to make sure what you are doing is on course to achieving your desired results.

Julie Hogbin has created a new Goal Setting system for the 21st century called STRUCTURE to meet the enhanced needs of the current age. The STRUCTURE system is as follows:

- **S**ystem to record and monitor goal setting.
- **T**arget which is measurable.
- **R**elevant linked to your vision and reason.
- **U**nderstand the pros and cons of the goal.
- **C**ommunicate effectively to self and others.
- **T**ime by when and how long.
- **U**nderstood by others.
- **R**eview regularly for progress tracking.
- **E**valuate to celebrate progress and to learn.

This comprehensive and encompassing system reflects Julie's years of experience and knowledge in business and she goes through the STRUCTURE system in detail in her book *Goal Setting - The Practical 'How to' Guide.*

What are your core values going to be?

Your core values are the values which define you and your business. Most businesses have agreed their core values and their work is aligned with, radiate from and centre around them.

> **If your values are unclear your message will be confused.**

They need to be very defined and could help you to target your ideal customer and to make your business stand out more to the right type of person for your business. If your values are unclear your message will be confused. What you do must align with your message and your values.

For instance, if you were looking for products to use or sell through your business and one of your core values is your business aims to safeguard the environment then you would want environmentally friendly products.

Having a business plan

While good mentoring can help keep you on track and focused on your business as well as providing someone to be accountable to, having a plan to follow will make it much easier for you to identify specific areas you need help with. A more structured plan will be needed if you need to borrow money. Online templates will help you to structure your plan and to make sure you know how you want your business to progress. Your plan will cover different sections:

- Why there is a need for your business. The type of business it will be, who you will be serving and how you will help them.
- Any research including what other competition is out there and the expected demand for your desired business.
- Work out your strengths and weaknesses to highlight

areas where you will need more help or knowledge.

- How will your business be organised? Where you will be and if you have a team who will be doing what? You can still create the roles and what tasks the person doing them will be responsible for even if it is you doing them to start.
- How you will run your business including marketing and sales.
- What will the financials be? What it is going to cost you, what you think your sales will be, profits and loss etc.
- A summary for others reading your plan so they can understand what it is your business does and how much money you expect it to generate etc. While this is shown at the beginning of your plan, it is best to write this part last.

Time specific plans

Using a time frame can help you to plan day to day activities. For instance, you could set yourself a certain goal to achieve in 90 days. You then work backward from the end of your goal, (day 90) to work out what you need to do from day 1 to day 90 in order to make it happen. Each month, each week in turn will be broken down into daily tasks. The actions achieving the best results for your business in terms of results such as generating income, should always take priority in any given working day and be done during your most productive times.

> **You'll know exactly what you need to be doing for you and your business.**

Your plan will be in sections or stages. To start, your short-term plan should run for a year and normally breaks down into 90 day sections or quarterly goals. The overall yearly plan will have the main objective such as to have x numbers of clients or customers or to create a certain amount of income. In each quarter you break it down into smaller goals which aim to achieve the larger one for this period of time.

By having a relevant plan with specific goals or tasks set for each day, each week, and each month means as you go along you can adjust areas to suit your needs. You'll know exactly what you need to be doing for you and your business; it will give you the focus and impetus for each day. Some people find this a very useful way to work because it gives them a defined structure to follow. Some areas of your business could have separate strategies or plans for specific areas such as your social media.

Creating your ideal Avatar

What kind of people do you want your business to attract? This is where you need to carefully consider your Avatar. Some people refer to this as a Persona. This is the blueprint if you like of your ideal customer or client. Your Avatar should also align with the core values of your business, so the people you attract to it understand what it is about and have a stronger interest and desire to engage with the products and services you sell. These are the people you want to be doing business with. The more you know about them the easier it will be for you to focus and plan other activities in your business. Your marketing and branding needs to appeal to your ideal customer and clients.

Research into the type of person you want to engage within your business.
- What do they do?
- Where do they work?
- Where do they shop?
- What age and sex are they?
- Where do they live?
- Are they in a relationship?
- Do they have children?
- What are their hobbies and interests?
- What type of music do they like to listen to?

- What issues and problems will they have which you can help to solve or what in their life can you help with to make it even better?
- What are their finances like?
- How do they like to spend their money?
- How do they spend their day?
- What times do they like to work?
- What are their aspirations?

The more you can create a vivid and detailed picture of this person, the more focused you will be at engaging with them. It will also help you to create a strategy for your plan so what you do is aimed at attracting and engaging with the right people for your business. It may even help you to define your core values and the bigger vision you have for your business better as well.

Alternative ways to plan

Even if you are a more organic person in terms of your thought processes or working practices, you still need to have some sort of structure to your day or for those specific tasks you need to complete particularly if they are time sensitive. Never put yourself in a position where you are trying to complete work at the last moment because you didn't plan your time more effectively or worse still failing to meet an important deadline.

> **A good plan, vision, dream, goal is never static.**

There are different ways to approach planning and remember you can include other activities as well. Some people like to use a diary, some use online programs or spreadsheets to create their plan. You could even do vision boarding to create a plan if it suits you better especially if you're a very visual person. A friend of mine, Michelle Chambers, has an amazing system for vision boarding which incorporates a structure you can follow to complete tasks and to progress your business. She also encourages you to include activities you enjoy doing for yourself.

Ultimately your plan should excite you. You should be viewing it daily, making regular changes and updates to it. A good plan, vision, dream, goal, or whatever you want to call it is never static. It has energy and a flow.

Having and running a business shouldn't be all about the business. A well-balanced person gives time for themselves. Remember to give yourself some time off, to have breaks, and to step back and recharge. Each day make a note of what you have achieved no matter how small you think it is. Always find a positive and worthwhile part of your day. By recording even the little wins, when you look back you'll realise you have done and achieved so much.

You may want to consider long-term goals for your business. A long-term plan could be 5 or 10 years even and will be less detailed. Your long-term plan holds the 'bigger picture' or your aims for you and your business. It still needs to be realistic, although there's no harm in adding an outrageous dream which scares or excites you! Again, as with your short-term plans, your longer-term plans can be tweaked and changed.

- What size business do you want to have?
- What will you do if you've not got as many clients and customers as you would like and want more or how will you cope if there were more custom than you can deal with?

Too much custom and you will need to expand and for some of you, your plan may be to expand in the future. Expanding a business can bring lots of issues, particularly when you're bringing in employees to work for you. Take advice and guidance from people who are or have been in this position and really understand and know what you need to do.

Why wouldn't you expand? The perfect situation for some of you is you have the exact number of people you need to run your business and you don't need or want anymore. Some people will be happy and will leverage the demand for their services or products to increase prices. Their focus will be their exclusivity. You should definitely leverage it if your niche is in a specific area and you're good at what you do.

Will your plan contain contingencies for unforeseen events happening? If your business literally relies on you then it has to be absolutely certain nothing can stop or disrupt it.

When you should step out and seek help

People often fall into scenarios where time is spent struggling to do tasks they don't like, don't enjoy doing or where the time would be better spent doing other tasks. Often or not, you're telling yourself it will cost too much to let someone else do it for you and you may also believe you can't afford it. Many people have this problem. What you may not realise, by having someone do the task for you (employment or outsourcing), it will free your time to do more important tasks.

Reasons to have other people doing tasks for you:
- It could save time and free you up to do the activities which create money for your business.
- They could do a better job of it and save you time and money.
- There's no shame in having help.
- You're wasting time doing the tasks you hate.
- You struggle to do the activities in which you're less skilled.

For instance, hiring a Virtual Assistant (VA) for time consuming admin tasks is quite simple and even if you start with an hour or 2 each month it should be worth your while. Make sure there is a contract so everyone understands and knows what is expected of them.

Do you have a partner or business partner who is resilient to change or who believes paying other people to do work tasks which you could do yourself is a poor idea? Often or not, they do not realise how it could serve your business better in the long term. You are all the sum of your own set of experiences and the views which come with them. As the business grows, you'll start to understand it needs to be approached in a very different way.

Multiple streams of income

Some people rely on one stream of income, but if you look at successful and wealthy business people, they will all give similar advice: You should have more than one stream of income; you should save and invest your money wisely, and you should always be looking to increase your value.

You never know how your business is going to change and your plan should be flexible enough to deal with this. I had an extra income to complement the business and it was going really well. When the company decided to change the protocols and the products, suddenly the income significantly dipped.

Additional sources of revenue are a good idea because they give you another product to rely on especially during leaner months. Multi-Level Marketing (MLM) is a popular choice for people who are still working, and some people do this until they have built a business with enough revenue so as they can leave the day job. The point is you are investing in market ready products. All you need to do is sell them.

> **To meaningfully incorporate other products into your business they should be congruent to you and your values.**

Another bonus is you are offering the people you deal with in your business a different and unique service or product from what they could buy in the shops. There are many companies and models out there. Do your research before signing up with any company to make sure you understand the structure of how it works, what outlay you need to make and if you will have certain targets you have to meet each month. Some companies or uplines in MLM do make you feel that to meet targets you have to make a significant spend each month. Some are very pressured.

I've never gone into companies where you've got to buy products each month or feel you are pressured to do so. You should only be spending what you choose to.

If you use and enjoy the products, you'll be more invested in the brand and you'll naturally build up and grow a business and if you choose wisely, it will complement and enhance your main business. To meaningfully incorporate other products in your business they will need to be congruent to you, your values, and fit your way of doing business. The MLM model and the system you choose needs to match you and your business, otherwise you'll find it very hard to make it work in terms of time and effort. Look at the support you are receiving.

My upline for dōTERRA encouraged me to take their Essential Oil Specialist Course to help expand my understanding of the oils and how they are made. It's useful having someone who's there to answer questions too, while other training, not only specific to the products, share skills which can be utilised in the business. I'm able to use these wonderful oils through the business with people in a natural and genuine way, but also it means they are being offered another product.

Open yourself up to other income streams and ways in which they can serve you, your business, and your valued clients and customers better. There are lots of other ways to create revenue, but whatever you choose it shouldn't be a distraction from your main business or cost you too much time or money to set up unless it will give you financial rewards in the long term.

People will pay for better

If you become too comfortable with what you charge and forget to plan for price increases you will be decreasing your value. Price increases reflect your growing experience and expertise along with increasing costs you will be paying year in year out. I've heard of practices which are overrun with customers, to learn they haven't changed their prices for years and years. People aren't necessarily looking for the cheapest, but the best value and will pay for better. People loyal to your business will stay because they know you and the product and services you provide.

Your plan may include the introduction of new products and services for the business as it expands. There is always room for improvement in any business with areas to tweak and change to keep it relevant and up to date. You would need to be extremely niche, to be giving only one service, and to survive without making any changes at all. You can carefully plan how to promote new products and services to build up interest before they are launched. You could also use people loyal to your business as test subjects and for feedback or testimonials.

Whatever your plan is, the aim of it should be to give you a structure and goals to follow with a business giving you the income and revenue you want, meaning you have the money to live the life you desire under your terms.

5: Knowledgeable People Let Their Customers Find Them Easily

Marketing is really important, it's purpose is to bring you new business and attract the right type of client. Information falling into the arena of marketing are mentioned in other chapters of this book, but you may want to seriously consider writing a separate plan encompassing this area. Marketing as a whole covers these 5 key areas:

- Advertising.
- Promotion.
- Publicity.
- Public Relations.
- Sales.

For example, to advertise an event you put up a notice telling people about it and to promote it you give out some flyers. For extra publicity, you do an interview in the local press about your event and to say you are donating to a particular charity. People are touched by your story (public relations). At the event, people come to you and you have conversations where you explain your products, how much they will help them, what a great investment they will be making, and how they will make their life better (sales).

Marketing is the process which brings all these elements together and for it to be a success you must have a strategy (the bigger picture planning), tactics (how you will get it all done), and a budget, which you can increase when you have tested and measured to see what works.

The more people who know, like, and trust you, the more likely it is they will engage with you, your business, and the products or services you sell.

I'm Here

Keeping your business visible

Networking and social media are a very powerful way of putting the message out there about you and your business. Advertising (adverts) are another valuable way of doing this and it isn't only about letting people know about your business, but can also help you to promote your products and services.

> **If your business fades into the background**
>
> **and is forgotten you will miss**
>
> **out on valuable custom.**

During leaner times and in more competitive markets your business must remain at the forefront of the minds of your target market and the people you aim to serve. If your business fades into the background and is forgotten or looked over you will miss out on valuable custom.

You need to target your niche and your Avatar(s). There are many ways you can advertise, but it needs to be relevant. Think of where or how your ideal customer is going to find out about you. Where will they look? For what reason are they looking? Your advert or message will in some way shape or form resonate with them, their needs and desires. If you are going to advertise it needs to serve a purpose. Placing lots of adverts, but with no real aim will simply be a waste of money. If you have good content it can bring new leads.

Using social media? Fine, but if you're not sure on the best way to do this take some advice from an expert, split test, experiment and then increase your spending.

Not all adverts are about selling. There's a difference between the type of advert you would put on social media to those you put online. Most people on social media are browsing for fun, to catch up with what is going on and less so for specific items to buy. If you want to use social media your presence there is more about growing awareness and getting noticed.

In fact, it's unlikely those types of people are ready to buy right now. It's about promoting your business to find the right people, letting them know you and your business is there to serve their needs.

Once people are aware of you and are engaged then you can start to draw them in. You may want more engagement from them. Will you be growing an email list? Perhaps you'll be offering a short e-book with some free content which targets a particular problem you are helping your chosen market to address and using this to ask for their email. Growing a mailing list means you can engage with people further through email or newsletters and when done well it can be very effective. It also means you can promote and offer your products, services or special offers.

People who are searching online are actively looking; for specific or additional information. Chances are if you are advertising online, you will be directing traffic to your web page. This should be functioning correctly, look professional, and any links are relevant and go to the right page. If you get it wrong it could become a very costly exercise. Do it right and you'll have good business through it. You will need to do some background work to set it up correctly as well as monitoring how your adverts are performing.

When deciding to pay for online adverts, as with social media, run a split test, you will need to experiment with wording before increasing your spending. If this is very new to you, take good advice and ask for help because it could save you time and money in the long term.

Looking to place adverts to reach people in your local area? Local businesses are often advertised in little booklets delivered to specific areas. This may be perfect for your business and older people often prefer to look for businesses this way.

Keep an eye on where your budget is going

If you don't watch where you are walking, chances are you may trip up. With marketing you need to keep a close eye on where the money is being spent or you may find you trip up because you have committed yourself to more than you can afford.

To start your marketing budget will be higher, but once you have established custom it can be from 1% to 10% of gross income, but you will need to know what you expect your Return On Investment (ROI) to be and as with all good plans do your research. Record where your referrals are coming from. There is no point in spending money on advertisements if where you are advertising is not reaching anyone. You can't measure what you don't know. Test to see what works well and then expand.

One year I wanted to increase the presence of the business and happened to start getting phone calls from people offering advertisement space in magazines going into doctors' surgeries and hospital waiting rooms etc. Promises were given such as lots of people would see the advert and how other businesses had benefited. There seemed to be no harm in signing up as they were going to help with the advert design and it was going to places where there was potentially new custom. There were more and more calls seemingly about the one or two adverts already placed, talking about the same points and it started to be confusing.

Being caught off guard, distracted and busy when the calls were made there came the sobering realisation; I had been saying, "yes" to lots of different opportunities and signed up for more than the couple of advertisements. It was a costly mistake. The worst realisation was none of the adverts actually returned any custom because they weren't reaching the right people.

Your advertisements wherever you place them should be relevant to your business. Don't waste space on unnecessary points which don't matter. Make sure your message is clear, focus on a specific service you provide and how it either helps with some sort of pain or gain for your target audience. Aim to catch the attention of the right people for your business. Don't clutter or confuse your message by trying to list or say all you do.

> **Make sure the 'call to action' is clear.**

The next most important point is how do people get in touch with you once they realise they need help? It's imperative for potential customers to find you quickly and easily and know how to get in touch with you. Make sure the call to action is clear. Shout it out! If it's a big banner at the top of the page on your webpage put it in a different colour so it really pops and grabs the attention of people. It's easy to become distracted, so don't let people be confused or struggle to find where the contact number or the link to get in touch with you.

In the local magazine the fonts on my advert were getting distorted because the sizing of the advert itself kept being changed. No one knew it was a problem until a customer said it was really difficult to read the phone number. They were right. The advert was adjusted with clearer fonts for the contact numbers and instructions were given not to alter the sizing of the advert in subsequent publications.

Some people like lots of shoes

You may or may not know someone who has lots of pairs of shoes for all sorts of occasions and to match different outfits. Then you may also know someone else who seems to live in one pair of shoes only. Some people just love choice. In business if you can have services showcasing different price frames it will help people to understand the value of what you offer and give them a choice also.

Shoe Shop

Have you noticed some garages and car dealerships where vehicles are serviced offer packages where there are different prices dependent upon the level of service you book your car in for? Basically, it is there to give you a comparison for each type of service on offer. It's not only about the cost being higher or lower, it's helping you to make an informed decision about what to have done on your car and it gives you a value and price frame as well. Some people will want all you offer and will be happy to pay more as they feel it is the better option, while other people won't.

If you only have one service with one price, there's nothing to make a comparison against or to choose from or more importantly to upgrade to.

The lure of a bargain treatment

Some people may compare the cost of your services with those of other service providers. On the surface it may seem they receive more from paying less and the beauty industry is one area where you may be familiar with this. The profit or extra money comes from the sale of high-value luxury brands demonstrated by and used in the treatment.

Let's take a facial as an example. The person doing the facial is telling you what they're putting on your face, what it does, how much better your skin looks and is asking if it feels any better. Then they'll say you should be doing this every day or once a week, how simple it is to do. All you need is to give yourself 'x' amount of time and continue a routine of looking after your skin using this particular product. There could be some further benefits as to why the product is good for you tied into issues and problems you may be experiencing with your skin.

> **The more a customer enjoys the experience you offer, the more likely it is they will spend more, remember you and use your services again.**

It is a sale, but you haven't paid a huge amount for the treatment itself, rather you paid to listen to and experience a long demonstration. At the end, they will try to persuade you to buy some or all of the products used on you during the treatment; this is the real cost. No doubt you will be told there is a special offer if you buy the set. Remember, the more time you spend with someone the better the rapport will be but only if your expectations have been met.

It can be a very successful model particularly if you know how to do it well and you accept some people will be happy to pay for the cheaper treatment, but without buying any of the products. This is why it is important to attract as many of the right people who will pay for extras through your door.

The more a customer enjoys the experience you offer, the more likely it is they will spend more, remember you and use your services again.

Can you make money by spending no money?

You may think the ideal marketing situation is where you don't have to spend money at all to interest new customers.

Word-of-mouth can be very powerful, although it relies on the person giving information in the right way to the right person. This could be a combination of leads from people met through networking and by creating a good rapport with people using your business.

Positive feedback should always be utilised as this is in effect free publicity which demonstrates good public relations. Let other people know you have satisfied customers. Start the habit of asking people if they are happy with the service you have provided. Ask if they can recommend you and always ask for positive reviews and testimonials as well if you can. Encourage and remind people to follow you on social media and to put reviews there. Ask if you can take a picture with them to put on social media. Again, you can tag them in, and they're sure to comment too. If your business is providing a service for the community then you can share details about this as well.

However, if you only pursue word of mouth as a means to promote your business, you'll be missing a lot of people who potentially could have been targeted through paid advertising who would have been actively searching for a solution to their problem.

When the business started, a lot of the early customers weren't online and there were some who could have given referrals via word of mouth, but weren't asked to. There were people who were perfectly happy with their treatments to recommend me to their friends, but weren't being pushed enough or asked to do this. The other problem is people did recommend and share the clinic's details, but the person they gave them to do not take any action even when reminded.

It's the same with online reviews. Some people don't need to be asked, but others need to be given permission, encouraged and reminded to do so, and told where and how they should do it. Not everybody is online or is comfortable giving an online review. You could ask for a written testimonial or card or give them a template to fill in. You could do a post online detailing how you did x treatment or service with someone who was very satisfied, share what they said, and describe how they said it made them feel. It's still a valuable testimonial in an informal sense albeit not as good as if the person had given their own testimony using their words. It is good to keep information up-to date, real and truthful in order to give people an idea about you and your business.

Regular posts and updates about you and your business in your social media keep it engaging for anyone who is browsing and sees it. They will think your business is more active than a page where the last post was months or over a year ago. Let people know what you do, what your service is, and how it can help them. Don't expect them to know. What's obvious to you won't be obvious to the people viewing your page. People buy into people. Use your social media to give a more personal side to your business.

I put some videos on my clinic page, a new customer watched one and said she was expecting it to be about feet, but it gave an unique viewpoint. She liked the video because it was more personal and a bit different. It reassured her to know she was coming to see a human being.

Blogs or free content are another great way to create engagement, rapport, showcase your knowledge and willingness to help as well as to create custom or new leads. People don't always buy straight away. Some need time to learn more about you before making a decision. Whatever you do you will need to be consistent, whether you use adverts or decide to do regular posts, having a presence on your social media and through other content.

People won't remember the one advert you put out, or the one email you sent, and they won't be able to find it when they do need your services. It's the same with your content. You need to be persistent with your posts particularly if you are running a campaign to promote a product or service in your business. With so much information readily available you need to stand out and be memorable.

Ultimately, with marketing, you want to attract the attention of those all-important new customers to buy from you and if you get it right, they will be returning regularly to use your services. If you're not getting enough customers or enough of the right customers, then you need to revise your message to make sure you are reaching the right people. Marketing is an art, it's an important area for your business, if you don't understand how it applies to you then take a course or ask for help.

6: Crazy People Want Things They Don't Need

As a cat lover and owner, I think I'm entitled to be a little bit crazy sometimes, but in business it isn't necessarily the best or most productive way to behave particularly when it comes to making decisions.

To start out there will be products, apps and services necessary for your business to operate, but often or not it is too easy to get carried away and to have more than you need. No business is perfect from the start and wasting your time, energy, and precious cash on items which simply are not urgent will not proactively serve your business. Business cards, logos and some equipment are relevant and have their place, but only when they serve the purpose to give you value. Listening to and learning from the people who matter to you the most, such as mentors alongside the people you serve in your business will guide you to make better and more informed decisions about what you really need.

Do you have preconceived ideas?

At the start of the business, I was treating myself as A.N. Employee and definitely wasn't thinking as a business owner should think. This is a common mistake for less experienced people to make. Decisions were guided by preconceived ideas of what was needed for the business, but without really thinking how those items would realistically be utilised.

Perhaps you have this notion when starting a business you need to get yourself a load of business cards. It's not necessarily bad practice to get a load of business cards as they have their place and uses.

An Electronic Business Card (also known as digital, virtual or E-business card) is basically an electronic or digital version of a paper business card and has the potential to hold more information about you and your business. There are simple apps to help you create one.

Electronic cards mean you can easily exchange your details and links to your different social media platforms through your mobile phone etc. There are still people though who like to have a physical business card, preferring to be given something real, enjoying the interaction of giving and being given a card, the sensory experience, of touching and looking at it, along with the conversation occurring during the exchange.

Whether it's a physical card or a simple electronic one it should have at the very least your basic details, your name, what you do, contact information, phone numbers, email and details of your webpage. On an electronic one you will have relevant links to your webpage and social media. It hasn't got to be as complicated as you imagined.

Physical cards can also include a QR code (short for Quick Response code) which is surprisingly easy to set up. These are the box-shaped barcodes in a pattern and you can scan them using a camera on any smart phone. They contain a link to information such as your webpage for instance. NFC tag reader (short for Near Field Communication tag reader) and other technology are going to dominate business marketing and communications in the future so be aware of the ways you can utilise them with other new technological advances in all areas of your business.

Having a basic web page is useful for your business because it gives you and your business a credible presence and will be necessary particularly if you're going to be running advertisements (ads) online and directing traffic there. If you are selling through other platforms, they often prefer you to have a webpage also because it adds credibility to your business. If your webpage is run and set up well it can give you a greater online exposure, reach and advantage.

What's in a name?

What other points do you think might be really important? You need to get a logo, right? I thought the business couldn't be started until it had a logo. For three whole months after qualifying there was the wait for the logo to be done.

> **For a business to survive and grow you need to trade.**

It may have been a fear of starting the business itself and here was an excuse because a friend offered to do the logo. I then waited for the logo to be done. All the time you're not trading, you're not making money and a fundamental for a business to survive and grow is the need to trade.

You need to be finding customers and clients.

While the name of your business is important it doesn't matter so much at the start because what you think is a really good name to begin with may not be the name which fits with what your business values are and how it's going to be in the future. If you are still working out these details sometimes getting started will help you to define your message and name from the feedback you get early on. You may think you have a future-proof name and it suits what you want your business to be, but sometimes the action of doing your business can subtly change those perceptions.

There are companies who have transformed; choosing to work in different areas from their original business plan but have kept the original name because to change your business name once you have it can be complicated as it involves re-branding.

What I should have done was to start the business as soon as possible once qualified. Secondly, worrying about the name of the business at this point was irrelevant. It could have been done later along with the logo because in the early stages there wasn't a lot of custom anyway. You can decide and change your business plan as you go along. Remember you have three months to register your company with the HMRC. Don't forget to check the name you want to make sure it isn't trademarked as well.

What serves your business the best?

Choose the people you want your business to serve carefully. By adopting someone else's Avatar you may create problems for yourself.

At the end of the Foot Health Practitioners course at the college, Victor gave some business advice and this is where I picked up his Avatar. It's one of the biggest mistakes I made for the business because it put a notion in place; the business would only serve a certain type of person and only do a very limited service.

The Avatar described was for elderly people Victor was doing his treatments in his own business and the kind of problems encountered had bothered him over the years. He said on a visit if a client is sat by the fire and the fire is on, to ask the client to turn it off because it might get too hot while doing their treatment. He had a predominantly domiciliary-based practice so how relevant was it really to my business? It only served to put a fixed type of person and scenario in my mind.

What items or equipment do you need to start your business? Again, the suggestion was from someone else who probably based it on what someone else told them and so on. It's not done with bad intentions, but it never really suited the business because it was more clinic-based. You end up with bits and pieces you'll never really use. Leaflets or flyers were another point to consider.

> # In business do everything with a purpose.

The advice was people are starting their practices, but aren't advertising and so are struggling to find new customers. Victor, asked if they'd sent out any flyers because this was what he believed you should do. Yes, you need to get the message about your business out there, but the thought in the back of my mind was there would be a lot to post.

How many flyers do we use? A very small amount and none were ever posted.

In business do everything with a purpose, and the purpose of having anything is to use it. It is brilliant if you're going to have flyers or leaflets made for your business, if you are going to use them. A really basic flyer with your name, details on what your business is offering, your phone number, your email address and a webpage (if you have one) is great if it's going to be used as a productive tool to get your message out there.

The flyers I first had made for my clinic had a weak layout and needed a more compelling message.

With a flyer, you've got 'real estate' on the back where you can put information too. It's the same with business cards, the back doesn't need to be blank. Do you think you're saving a bit of money printing one side? Why don't you make use of the extra space if you will so the information is more spread out and easy to read?

How are you going to be distributing your leaflets or flyers? Are you going to post them? Ask yourself these questions and if you answer them honestly you may find you don't actually need them or want them or want the hassle of distributing them or finding someone to do it for you, which could be a costly exercise.

One of the reasons a flyer drop didn't happen for the clinic was because I wanted them to go through the letterboxes of people who would most likely be interested and needed to work out what streets would be the best to deliver them to. Then there was the time and the inclination to do it. In truth, my husband would have shoved them through any letterbox until they ran out.

Or it could be for what you're doing flyers are a brilliant and cost-effective way of finding new customers in your area, but you do have to think about the cost. There's no use in having thousands printed if realistically you're not going to need such a large amount just because it works out cheaper per item for a bulk order. It's like the multi-buy savings at the supermarket; it's not a saving if you never use it. You're only helping the supplier to offload their excess stock.

On occasion, we like to do a car boot. It's a chance to get rid of some unwanted items and make a bit of cash and it is fun standing your ground on price. We met a bloke there, Nick who's a pest controller. He goes around, sometimes in his work overalls looking for a bargain or two and if he strikes up a conversation and if it's appropriate, he hands out his flyer.

His flyer gives a good deal of information (front and back), but it's not fancy or excessive. We actually used him to get rid of a wasp's nest. At our house I asked him if he got much business from the car boot sales, he said he did. You see, Nick knows who his potential customers are and what they are interested in. No doubt people see the badge on his overalls, ask him about it; the subsequent conversation leads to him handing out his flyer.

Note: At the bottom of the flyer Nick's phone number is given –
not shown in the example.

*Leaflets were done for the clinic and these are a
great way of letting people know about your services.
I wouldn't say they get new custom, but they do
highlight to existing or new customers what other
services you provide especially if you are increasing
prices, making a significant change or adding a new
service. Some people like to have the information to
look at later on and to show to family members or
friends.*

> **Focus on what you physically need to**
>
> **do what you do in your business.**

Do you really need headed stationery printed for your
business? How often are you going to be sending actual
letters? Nowadays most people communicate via email etc.

*One of my friends made the headed letters and
compliments slips. These were done electronically,
which is excellent as you can easily do decent quality*

prints yourself. There have been letters sent from the clinic, but the compliment slips have never been needed.

A friend Gija Melnupe sent me a copy of her info booklet, *Pet Friendly Garden Design Guide*, with a compliment slip and it had a handwritten message on it from her. It made it more personal and it was congruent with her personality and her business.

If you need to do even a reasonable amount of printing get a decent printer. Very cheap ones are not a good economic buy in the long term because the cost to replace ink cartridges is high. You can refill ink cartridges, but look into this to make sure you are happy with the quality.

Things You Don't Need

You may decide you need to have a stationery container to put your pens and paper clips in, but how many times are you actually going to use a paperclip? Apparently, in the USA 11 billion paperclips are made each year. Who on earth is using them? Even in an office job I hardly ever actually needed to use one! You make up reasons with yourself on how much you will need all these bits and bobs, but think it through and ask yourself do you really need all these items right now?

What I actually needed to start my clinic was the physical room to start practicing in, some basic equipment and the furniture to facilitate treatments.

A lot of these ideas come from this premise; for a business to function it needs to have the fancy paper with your logo and details on, plus the compliment slips, the business card etc, but actually, it may not be necessary for you to have them all when you start out. Prioritise on what you need physically to make your business operate well.

In some ways, less is more because as your business grows, you can buy more equipment if you need it. Worrying about having lots of equipment, furniture and other bits and pieces isn't necessarily relevant unless you will use them.

Keep it simple because as you become more experienced you will learn you have your own preferences.

For instance, I don't like the type of probes used at the college and prefer a different type. It proves you don't have to copy. You can adapt to suit you.

If you have tools or equipment you don't need or don't use it will not only cost you, but they take up valuable space. Perhaps, you become sentimental and reticent about getting rid of items because you've paid for them. Trust in the experience, as you go along, you'll learn what you really need to make your business as efficient and as effective as possible. In this day and age, you can get items delivered very quickly and easily too.

7: Wise People Ask For Help

If you have ever struggled to do something and then when you finally asked for help the solution was so quick and simple you wished you had asked sooner then you'll understand why getting help for you and your business could be very useful.

> **You need to be comfortable utilising the knowledge and experience of others and be able to ask for help.**

Finding the right people to ask for help is key to having an effective business. Whether it's a mentor you're looking for or finding the right places to go to for advice, support or grants, you need to be comfortable utilising the knowledge and experience of others and be able to ask for help.

Do you want a mentor or a coach?

Engaging the services of a mentor will usually be more long term and you would expect a mentor to have more first-hand experience in your area of business, while a coach will be more about improving performance and follows a more structured approach. One of the best things you can do for yourself and your business is to get a mentor or coach and as long as you find the right person to help with your needs it should be very useful. You don't want to latch on to the first person who approaches you because they think they can coach or mentor you. Their experience and or expertise may not be relevant to your area of business and they may not be able to give you the best and or most productive advice. It's not about having a friend, but there does need to be some sort of rapport. You also have to consider how cost-effective it will be for you and your business.

Some mentors or coaches offer a free session for half an hour or so. This gives you a chance to have a little conversation with them to understand more about them, their experience and knowledge, if you like them and if you think you could work with them. If they are offering some value-added content via a blog or podcast for instance, go and listen to what they are saying and ask some questions. Some people do training days or taster sessions.

To start with you may not have a lot of funds available, but you could put mentoring or coaching to feature around your business plan and use the person you are working with to help you to get the plan started and set up. Most mentors and coaches would probably agree that more sessions to start are better, but if funds are really tight, arrange to meet up every quarter/90 days. Hopefully, in between each session, you'll have been able to take on board and implement the tasks and suggestions given to you. Those tasks should have given you some pointers to make sure you're gaining new business to generate income so you've got some money there for the next session.

> **A good coach or mentor can help you to grow your business.**

As your business grows you'll probably want to increase mentoring or coaching sessions to keep the momentum going. Remember you can change the people you work with to a more experienced one if and when necessary.

People often begrudge paying for coaching or mentoring, but a good coach or mentor can help you to grow your business.

Some sessions with my mentor Kerry Malster, ActionCOACH gave some really valuable focused advice and made me think about some weaker areas of the business. Through some of her suggestions and help something was added to a service in the clinic and in turn it significantly increased revenue. It was very simple but effective.

Sometimes you need another set of eyes on your business and someone to listen to your problems or concerns so they can hone in on the areas where improvements and changes can be made.

Group sessions are another option so long as they are well managed and run, they can be very beneficial and more cost-effective. Find out about the person running the group first. A good coach or mentor who resonates with you will take the time to look at your business and will understand what your needs are whether it is as a 1:1 session or as a group. Group sessions can have their plus points and some offer added value by sharing lessons and content on different areas of business. Do check to find out how large the group is, how it will be run and structured. Too large and there will be less time for you to receive more personal advice.

Don't make the mistake of joining an expensive business mastermind group on the back of an event as I did. With different people involved in leading the monthly mentorship sessions, there was no continuity. Some of the mentors were more experienced than others and there was no real structure or overall plan on how it was run. None of the mentors got to know about me or my business properly to offer decent advice.

If you still don't think coaching or mentoring is a priority or necessary, think again, especially if you really are new to business. Having someone who can give more informed answers and who you can sound out any ideas on processes and ideas you're thinking of trying for the business to is always useful. Chances are with their experience they will direct you to other people who can help too.

This could save you a lot of time and money in the long term. Keep your business up-to-date with any necessary Continuing Professional Development (CPD). For some professions it can be part of your insurance terms. Think about your own continued development and aim to do something each year as part of your business to help you to learn and develop with it. If you're keeping your knowledge current and up-to-date then you're less likely to fall behind. If you get too comfortable with what you know, but never actually grow your knowledge then someone else could easily end up stepping in and being seen as a better expert or having a better service. You'll need to keep up with current trends and learning as things change to remain ahead in your area of business.

Finding help for your business

Part of the fear of not asking for help for me especially at the start came from my upbringing and consequently, I missed out on many opportunities. Your background may hold you back and it comes from many different experiences and sources, some you've probably forgotten about, but are there deep in your psyche. You carry them into your adult life and it affects how you behave and react to situations. You then tell yourself it is easier and safer to say or do nothing or you behave in a way which can be misconstrued.

I started my business as A.N. Employee carrying fears from the embarrassment to ask questions or to put myself out in front of people because when I'd tried to do so in the past, in my childhood, in the workplace or anywhere else it had been a very uncomfortable, unhappy and negative experience.

Now in awkward situations, I try to step back, observe and take advice before making decisions, or doing or saying anything because in business your actions need to be the best for it in the long term.

When you start your business do have a look to find out if there are any grants or funding available. There are funds which you can apply for, it's a case of knowing where to ask, who to ask to help you in order to make it possible for you to make an application. You will need to carefully read the details to ascertain if you are eligible, if there are any conditions attached to the grant but be aware grants are taxable. Applying can be a chore, but it is still worth a try.

If you need advice or help, consider joining your local Chamber of Commerce or The Federation of Small Businesses. They offer support and advice to business owners and give huge value for money to their members with insurance, cover for jury service etc. Some universities give free support as well as access to meeting areas and other resources. Don't forget your Local Authority either. People you meet through networking could connect you to helpful contacts or potential investors as well.

> **Finding the right people to help you is key.**

It's the things you don't know when you start out which can make having a business harder for you. Finding the right people to help you is key. The right help and advice could save you and your business money or give the business valuable cash to invest back into it. I'd never heard of a Chamber of Commerce or knew what it did, but I discovered the answers through networking and my reason for joining may surprise you.

I've always used an accountant to do the accounts because the fear of getting anything wrong with the HMRC is petrifying. When younger and doing accounts and clerical work I would sometimes add numbers up incorrectly. Fred the accountant there would say, "You added this up wrong. How did you do that? It took me ages to find out what had happened and why it was wrong!" It would be 10p out; only a tiny amount, but it still needed to be correct.

It's absolutely essential to ensure your finances are correct and in order because if you make a mistake the HMRC could get involved.

Key to the Right People

If you don't trust yourself to deal with your own finances then the natural solution is to pay someone to do it for you and they'll do it right. For some people, the HMRC forms may seem complicated and overwhelming.

Once in a group mentorship meeting I attended, one of the mentees said the HMRC came to his business to check the accounts. It cost an extortionate amount of money (around £30K) to sort out even though they hadn't done anything wrong.

You may think it probably won't happen to you, but would you have the money to sort a problem like it if it occurred?

> **Ask and keep asking.**

I met Paula from the local Chamber of Commerce at a networking event and she dropped, ever so casually, into the conversation about one of the benefits you gain by being a Chamber member is having legal protection for the accounts. Having this legal protection makes the membership worthwhile, everything else provided with membership is a bonus. In fact, the membership would have been useful to have during the early days of the business because you can access courses, networking and other useful resources.

It's all about what you know already and what your existing background is. If you genuinely don't know or do not have any existing contacts who can help, you will need to consider how you can move yourself and your business forward. It's about learning to put yourself in front of other people, hopefully the right people who can help you and/ or those who can put you in contact with potential leads or help. Remember, you can ask and keep asking. Take good advice and don't rush into anything.

Business isn't just about the physical;

producing services or products,

it's also about getting you and your

message out there. It's like a dance.

8: People Who Learn The Business Dance Find New Connections

Hopefully, by now you're beginning to think about the variety of activity you need to be putting into place to make your business work. Business isn't just about the physical; producing services or products, it's also about getting you and your message out there. It's like a dance. You'll either enjoy it or endure it! Being part of a good network or having a consistent online presence can really help you and your business. You need to think about how you can make yourself visible in the wider community, become known and start building contacts. Two ways you may consider will be through in-person and/or online networking and by using your social media.

Step into networking

Your business may predominantly serve other businesses so building a good business-to-business (B2B) network early on will be key. How much and how often you're networking will depend on what you want to achieve from it and the type of business you have. If you want to build trust and rapport with people you need to be a consistent presence, you will need to plan this into your monthly or weekly activities. If your business is more a business-to-customer (B2C) format, networking may not need to be so dominant in your activities, but will still have value.

When you work alone in particular, networking can give you valuable contact outside of your business with the

You don't have to Climb Mountains

chance to share any wins or problems you may be facing with fellow business people who will always be happy to offer advice and support.

On a more basic level, networking gives you the chance to say who you are, what you do, who you can help, and any areas you need help in. If you network well the people you make contact with could lead to collaborations with their businesses, they might recommend you to other businesses people and their contacts or become customers of your business, which is why networking can be very beneficial. Target your message to the right people and you'll get a lot out of it.

It also emphasises why it is important to make the right impression and to have a memorable message. The growth of online networking has opened up the possibilities and reach of networking as well. My publisher, Ladey Adey has written a fabulous book about networking, *Successful Business Networking Online*, it's a good resource to learn the value of networking for your business.

> **You don't have to climb mountains**
>
> **to find the right people.**

Starting out in networking can be a bit daunting and if it is new to you it may mean you will have to step out of your comfort zone. Once you have got the hang of it, you'll find it a lot easier. So, how do you do that?

Firstly, you'll need to find some networking groups that suit you and your business the best. Membership-only groups in particular usually offer one or two free sessions so you can decide if the group is right for you. It means you don't have to climb mountains to find the right people!

Membership groups may have criteria for joining as well. For instance, some groups won't have more than one type of business represented - a lockout policy, to give more variety in the types of businesses. Taster sessions will help you to understand how a particular group is run and what is expected of you. Some people use very structured groups as a type of mentoring or coaching because they give goals and encourage you to fulfil certain tasks between each meeting. You may have some form of value-added content offered and if you are a regular attendee of a group, you could be asked to do a talk around your area of expertise. Some groups encourage you to introduce new people into it, which helps to keep the dynamics livelier and more interesting.

You usually have an opportunity to give your business pitch, which is a really effective way of talking about you and your business. Also, you'll be sharing how your services could potentially help people in the room, if you're looking for certain types of businesses or people in the room to work with, to use their services, or for recommendations.

Save the waffle for breakfast

The area which drives me crackers about networking is the 'waffle' and I'm not talking about the type you eat! These are the people who don't know when to stop or how to convey their message in the most effective and efficient way. If you haven't prepared what you're going to say, a 60-second pitch quickly becomes 2 minutes or longer and turns into a meandering confusing rhetoric. You know you love your product; you love your business and suddenly it's like you're reciting a shopping list of everything you do and offer. In larger groups there isn't the time for this and you may find yourself being cut off in your prime if you start rambling on for too long. If you miss sharing a crucial point you wanted to make, it may mean you could have missed out on an important opportunity. The other point about your pitch is if it's short and sweet people will remember it and you better. This means it will be easier for people to share your message with others.

Save the Waffle for Breakfast

Your minute pitch isn't about bamboozling people with lots of information. It's about giving a little taster or teaser if you like, to make you and your business a little bit tantalizing. Just think about your first date. You don't want to be going all out there for the first time. You want a bit of mystery and intrigue. You need to have a little bit of a mystique so people are curious and want to ask you more questions. You don't want them to be bored or confused by your message. It's the same if you are talking to different people in a room. The more concise your message is the more people you will be able to make contact with.

What could you say in your minute pitch? There are different formats out there. A simple one would be to give your name and your business name. If you haven't got a name for your business yet, you could say *"This is a brand-new business and we're still working out the details, but basically the business is..."* and then in a few short sentences summarize what your business is, what you do, who you want to serve and if you want any help, and so on.

If you're looking for certain help or connections you need to be concise about what you want. For instance, *"I'm looking for somebody with business experience who also does mentoring and has expertise in x area/ serving y type of people.* "Hopefully you'll get the person with relevant experience to suit your needs. Remember to reiterate your name and business name at the end of your pitch in case anyone didn't quite catch it at the beginning particularly if you are giving it to a room full of people. Remember, a minute pitch should be one minute so practice this.

Try and connect with as many people in the room and get their contact details or business card. Any viable leads should be followed up with an email or phone call as soon as possible afterward. Find people online as well and connect with them there. Don't leave it too long or they will forget who you are or you'll get distracted with other aspects of your business and it won't get done.

Exploring social media

With over 50% of the world's population using social media (2021), there is so much potential to raise your business profile, but is easy to get lost in it all. This number is rising each year as online activity expands and increases. Planning your content on social media is a good idea, but it is a wide topic and for different businesses, different types of social media will be more suitable. Whether it is visual, written, audio, to watch or interact with, there are many opportunities for you to share your message. If you have an aptitude for social media definitely start promoting yourself and your business. Even if it isn't your forte, seriously consider how this can fit into your business plan or outsource this part of the work.

The most popular platforms will be more widely known, used and have the greater reach and potential audience for you to tap into. Each platform has a different strength. This doesn't mean you can't use newer, less well-known ones, and these may be good to use if your target audience has a younger dynamic. Don't spread yourself too thin by being in too many places. Start off with one or two which suits your business the best and focus on getting them working for your business. Then expand into others. Whatever platform you use be aware of any rules about posting, content, and of any changes that might affect your business.

Create a meaningful connection

The purpose of social media is to create rapport and connection between people. It's about putting you and your message out there to let them know how and what you do and what your business is about, how it works, but also what you are doing right now in your business.

> **People remember how you made them feel.**

People love to see behind-the-scenes content, to hear about what you are doing, and to feel a connection. They want to understand your thought processes, learn more about your personality, your 'why' in business and to see another side to you. They can then decide if your business is one which they can interact with and relate to. You can also posit yourself as an expert in what you do.

People remember how you made them feel long after they have forgotten what was said or done and if someone was choosing a business, but wasn't sure, the one where they can identify with the people more and on a more personal level is most likely to grab their attention.

Show and share how you go above and beyond to help people. Keep it simple and to the point. Think of the pain points, problems or ways you can make life better for the people you are targeting in your business. How can you help them? When people see and understand that they're more likely to connect.

> **Get your social media right and potentially it can really help your business.**

Target people who you can serve the best and who will be more likely to engage with you and your business. Some businesses choose a blanket approach thinking more likes or followers is better. This is not strictly true. Others say go for quality leads not quantity. You'll have more post engagements and less hassle from the right people than from the ones who are not interested in you and are less likely to engage in your posts and content anyway.

Try not to randomly follow people because again it will attract the wrong type of interest to your page. Look at the profiles of the people who are actively and genuinely engaging in what you do, learn more about them, and further target your content to be more attractive to people like them who want to engage. Get your social media right and potentially it can really help your business. Utilise evergreen content too. This is content that can be shown any time of the year and you could repeat content at different times.

Potentially you could get support from existing friends and family especially if they are commenting on your posts in a useful and constructive way because comments and shares all boost posts so more people will see them. As a caveat consider carefully how you use social media and the different platforms for your business. Remember if you are inviting friends, family and other people who know you into this are they going to want to feel like you are selling to them or talking business all the time? It needs to be balanced and understandable.

There are platforms where you can have a business page, which can give you a wider range to explain what you do or give opportunities to run ads to your page. It means you can separate your business from your personal profile. The good point about this is you should get access to analytics so you can monitor and follow how your posts are performing and what types of posts get the most interactions.

Build a community

You could create groups as well, which you can then link to your business page. What's the difference between your business page and your group page or similar? Your business page is all about your business, new and existing products and your services. You'll be growing your brand, connecting with your customers, keeping them informed, and building up a community of followers.

> **The more people are aware of you and what you are offering the more you are going to be in the front of their minds.**

A group page is more of a niche community, usually has restricted access and rules governing what goes on in there. Group pages are where people who want more can join whether it's for extra content or special offers. Some people have groups with paid for access because they use them to give exclusive content. Whenever possible monitor the people in your groups, you can give questions they have to answer to join. Look at their profiles if you're not sure about someone. You will learn what a good or bad profile is through experience and common sense. You may not want people coming in to your group to sell their products or services for instance, which is why rules help to keep content appropriate.

You can schedule posts and content, which will involve a bit of pre-planning and time to do, but once you've done it you won't have to worry about posting every day. Also, it'll free you to share more organic content, post 'lives', highlight a special offer or talk in more detail to your followers. If you share regular valuable content hopefully people will be engaging with your posts. A really good group will have people posting content for you and will have lots of interaction, however, you will need to manage this.

Remember to interact with people if they comment on any of your posts because it can help push the post in front of more people. The more shares, comments, and interactions on a post the more people will see it. If you post regularly and consistently it's more likely you and your posts will be noticed. In smaller groups, the interactions may be less. Don't take it personally. Some people are happy to look and are absorbing information even if you don't realise it. Concentrate on putting out better quality. Just showing up and focusing on the people who do like the content you share will teach you a lot. Ignore anyone else.

The more people are aware of you and what you are offering the more you are going to be in the front of their minds when they do need to use you and your services or to recommend you to someone they know.

Walking on hot coals

When you share parts of yourself and your business you can become sensitive to perceived criticisms, but you need to learn from and strengthen yourself to deal with this. Sometimes you may think someone is questioning you, but it could be they need clarification.

I had this in one of my groups. A person was asking a lot of questions, but it turned out they had a genuine concern and wanted to make sure they were asking the right person about the particular problem they had.

Don't take it too personally or allow yourself to get angry or defensive because you've misinterpreted someone's intention. Learn to take criticism. Everyone has their own set of opinions based on their experiences and views of world, if someone's given a lot of time to interact by giving a response to your post then they're engaging with you.

Comments and criticisms aren't always meant to be hateful or personal in a nasty way; when it happens it is usually obvious. Could it be someone is trying to share their genuine and honest opinion if it's a criticism and you don't like it? Some people say they've had their first troll and when you read it if it is a post for instance, their comments give valid points and the person putting it there has actually put a lot of thought and energy into what they've said. Ultimately, it's their point of view and perspective on a given situation.

> **Show your genuine self.**

If you get criticism of your product or service and it's a valid one you have to take note. It can be upsetting when it happens. Just address it honestly. If it was a mistake admit it. People come from different viewpoints and it may be a simple change in what you do could stop any misunderstanding in the future.

Don't delete it or try to hide it because you need to show a little bit of transparency and people who know, like, and trust you will see it for what it is, also they may even come to your defence as well.

Sometimes people can be quite thoughtless in what they say because they post random comments on social media or in reviews without thinking about the consequences especially the impact it can have on a smaller business. Every little comment means so much and you want it to be positive, but you have to learn from what people say as well and then make sure you re-hone and improve for next time.

If you're showing your genuine self, you will find people will stick up for you if someone is persistently being disruptive or rude. Some will reach out and message you in person. You can control this eventuality. You can block or ignore people who are particularly venomous and negative.

Trolling when you see it, is usually nonsense. All they are going to do else is fill your time and feed you with their negativity.

I belong to a business-related group and set myself a challenge to put a post in there every single day for 90 days. A small number of people, mainly men, clearly had issues with the post content going into the group. One, in particular, had taken it upon himself to police it. Now, this is his opinion and what was confusing was why he spent so much time commenting on the posts he didn't like.

There will be people who are just idiots, enjoy spite and hide behind a persona.

Interestingly, I've noticed the biggest critics often do not have a picture of themselves on their profiles. In fact, one of them was using an emoji as his social media profile picture, another one a logo but neither showed their faces. They were hiding behind an image!

> **Only comment on posts you think**
>
> **are appropriate.**

What can you do? You don't have to engage with the comments of trolls. Alternatively, you can treat their comments with humour.

All I did was to put the laughing emoji on their comments, which took minimal effort for me and was probably very irksome for them to see.

Someone I know took it upon himself to address every negative comment made about him in a post because he believed the people concerned needed to be educated with the facts.

It's up to you how you deal with it and if it's someone else's group you are contributing on it is the responsibility of the administrator to monitor and control the content.

My advice is this. Only comment on posts you think are appropriate, align with your values or views, or that you're comfortable with, unless you want the interaction. The truth is you don't know what's going to get the traction and responses. You're learning what is and what isn't working, what gets a reaction, and what gets none. Some people like controversy because lots of responses and interactions keep a group livelier.

What you may not know or notice is your method of communication can also affect people. Too many question-type posts can be tiresome. It can be easier to do these and yes you may have interactions, but as a long-term strategy, it can get wearing especially if the questions begin to sound desperate, trite or negative.

Who's to say what is a good question and what's a bad question? Is a good one the one getting lots of responses or is it a cleverer question maybe with fewer or none? Just think of it this way, if you're getting comments on your posts, you're getting noticed. Why would someone waste their time on a post they think is rubbish? If you want to be taken more seriously though try to give good variety. Show your personality, your expertise, share tips and mix it up with different types of content.

If you have a visual product think of putting your message out on platforms where you can showcase it with good quality pictures. If it's not your gifting, if the lighting is poor or if you don't have a very creative eye your images will be remembered for the wrong reason. Get photographs done by a professional especially if it saves you time and makes it look better. Product and lifestyle shots don't have to be expensive.

A lot of platforms have links so people can click on a picture and buy the product. Make sure all your links are correct as well. Take advantage of what is out there and what is best for your business. You can utilise free stock images for your social media too where relevant.

Social media when done well can be time-consuming. You may have a dedicated person doing this later on, but until then work out a consistent system that works for you.

Blogging and/or Vlogging is another great way to interact with people and again you can schedule them so you don't have to worry about creating content daily. Blogs are your written content while Vlogs are video-based and are often used to demonstrate or show something. Both when done correctly can increase your reach through search engines. If you've got a Blog on your webpage and you regularly add content to share your expertise, it may help expand the reach of your web page.

Good quality content can build up your brand and you can re-purpose it on other platforms. A blog for instance could be broken down into different types of smaller content and this can be used on your other platforms. Not only can it increase your reach, but will save you the time of having to create new content on each platform. It involves planning and structure, but can be very effective and will keep your content and message consistent.

Have a valued presence

People aren't just going to find you on social media. Having a webpage for your business will make you more visible professionally and can also bring potential customers to your business. People need to be confident that you are who you say you are when you start out. Your webpage gives you and your business a valued presence. Your web page doesn't have to be complicated but you want to make an impact.

Keep your website simple, when you have some money flowing into the business then arrange for a more professional page to be done. Use original photos of you in your business, original images by a photographer, rather than stock pictures as this looks more personal and genuine. Show what you are doing to create a brand of yourself and your business. Your webpage should be clear and easy to use, with information on how people can get in touch with you, where you are, what you do, who you serve and help. If you are selling products through your webpage, make sure the pictures are clear and the process for taking payment is as easy as possible. Keep your site secure and remember you may have to pay to keep a particular domain name for your business.

With existing customers, you can create extra rapport by sending out a monthly newsletter. It's quite easy to set up, then you can chop and change content quite easily each month. You can even put video links in there, which adds another dimension to your content and another way of communicating with people because everyone absorbs information in different ways. Have links for people to sign up for your newsletter through other platforms as well.

Liven it up

Perhaps, you could set up your own podcast to expand your audience and reach. Even if you don't like the sound of your own voice, you'll be surprised by how other people hear you. People enjoy listening to other people speak and consume content through listening. You can get transcriptions done of your recordings and re-purpose the content on your other platforms.

> **'Live' and video content creates a connection with your audience and potential clients.**

Live content gives the chance for you to talk to your audience and can be more personal. It doesn't have to be slick, in fact, people love to see you as you are saying it how it is. If you get people engaging with you in your lives it will increase their reach. People often make excuses not to do 'lives' or video content. The best action is to 'just do it' even if you don't think it is the best time of day, or you don't think you look so good. People can't see everything. So long as your face and your shoulders look presentable people aren't going to know what's going underneath and it's better to do than not to do.

'Live' and video content creates a connection with your audience and potential clients. A simple tip to remember is to look directly at the camera. Whatever you use to do your 'live', work out where the camera is and learn to look at it. While it's tempting to watch yourself on the screen, for the viewer, it won't look like you are talking to them directly. Perceived eye contact is very powerful.

Remember, the more you move around the more it's going to show on the 'live' and subsequent video. For some people, it can be incredibly distracting and off-putting. I personally get quite giddy when a person records themselves while walking. If you are walking or outside, you'll need a gadget to steady your equipment or just stand still.

Think about lighting. Can people see you clearly enough? There's plenty of simple, light and easy to use set-ups which can easily be moved around. Learn to utilise natural light when you can, but be aware sunlight can be very harsh. Don't have too much clutter behind you either because some people are intrinsically nosey and that half-eaten pizza or your shopping bags are a distraction.

Make sure the sound is clear. Some people use a clip-on microphone. If you're out and about try and find a quieter spot. In the home or office turn off any background noises such as the TV, radio, or washing machine.

Not everybody is listening. Maybe they're just scrolling through content and looking at whatever comes up on their feed so you'll need to do something to grab their attention. Remember people absorb their content in lots of different ways. Simple applications (apps) can add the transcription/subtitles of what you are saying so people can read as they view if they're not listening to the sound.

If you are nervous about doing live or recorded content, you'll find the more you practice the more confident, proficient and efficient you will be. If people can relate to you as a person the greater the rapport with them will be. Have fun with your 'lives' and videos. If it goes wrong it doesn't matter. You don't have to keep it. Content is easy to create, change, and to delete if it isn't right.

If you are using social media as part of your strategy decide when you're going to be present on it so you get the maximum output from your input. Test the best times for your market and the people you are reaching out to. There's no use in posting or being present at 11am if the people you are trying to reach are more active at 8pm. Use the analytics available on a lot of platforms to work out what results you are getting from what you're doing. Scheduled content is great because you can have pre prepared content posted at the optimal times. If you're not clued up on social media and analytics then take a course on it at the very least.

Whose face is it anyway?

Your headshot is really important and is the face of you and your business. So, always have an up-to-date professional image of you on your website and social media profile. It's not wrong to have your logo instead of your face, but if you want your brand to feel more personal a good headshot of you is better.

> **People relate to people.**

I used to use my logo everywhere because it gave continuity. A logo begins your branding, but you're not quite at the stage of being a big brand name and having the kind of brand recognition when you start out whereby people know who you are through your logo. Now, I use a mix of headshots and my logo depending on the page or site it is on.

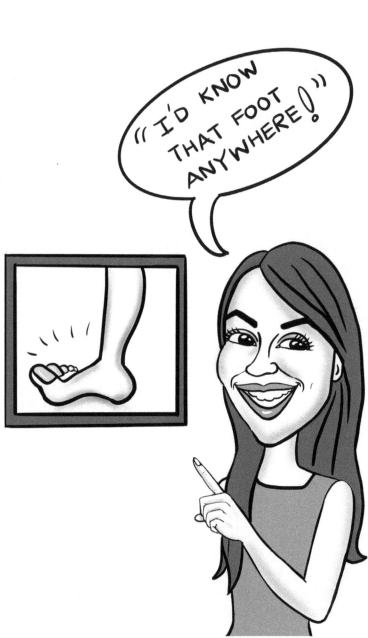

Whose Foot?

First and foremost, people relate to people. If you want your personal profile to be more personal that's fine, but keep the funny pictures away from your business profile especially if you want to be taken seriously. Pictures of you and your pets, your pets, a blurred shot of yourself on a drunken night out, or other inappropriate images as a profile picture may not put the best message about you and your business unless it's a dog and you're a pooch groomer. Sometimes the first contact a person has with you and your business is through your social media and online presence, this is where an opinion is drawn about you.

It's easy to get professional business photographs for your social media profile. Find someone locally or you're sure to find someone through networking. Photographers who do headshots for social media often price them very reasonably and you'll be supporting a local business in the process. There's no need to spend a fortune on pictures because you should be updating them every 1 or 2 years to keep your profile current and up to date.

Remember, there's nothing more disconcerting than an amazing profile picture, but when you meet the person in the flesh they do not resemble the person in their picture. Make sure your profile picture looks like how you look now and is reflective of who you are, how you look and the person people will be meeting in the flesh. Don't over 'glam' it by putting too much makeup on if you don't normally wear much or go overboard with filters. People want to see the real person; they don't want to have their expectations confused because the confused mind doesn't buy!

Social media takes time and energy to work. Enlighten yourself on the important posts which are going to affect you and your business. If you're not paying attention to it, then don't expect your social media platforms to work for you. Try to balance it out as well. Some people use a formula where they post particular types of posts on certain days. This gives structure to their social media and having a plan means you know where you are. It can be a bit obvious, but if it works for you then why not? Other people prefer to mix

A lot of people allow their business and personal finances to merge and forget to actually pay themselves.

9: Clever People Develop Good Habits

If you can introduce the habit of routinely doing work and pre-empt the activities you know are going to happen you will be a lot more prepared and organised in your business. Areas you can focus on are finances, price increases, and your personal development and growth.

> **Make a habit of paying yourself a sum of money from the start.**

Pots of money

A lot of people allow their business and personal finances to merge and forget to actually pay themselves. Make it a habit of paying yourself a sum of money from the start of your business and put in a separate account. Learn to increase the amount you pay yourself on a regular basis, this way you're helping to give yourself an income rather than all the money being absorbed back into the business.

You can have accounts or imagine different saving pots if you will for training, for personal development, for bills, taxes, etc, and again cultivate the habit of putting aside money or at least having a 'pot' or account where the money goes for these expenses.

It is very easy to tell yourself you are cash-rich because you think you have more money in your accounts than normal, when actually the money should have been earmarked to

Pots of Money

pay insurance costs or advertising and you've then spent it on something less important.

Monitor the steps of your cash flow

Do look at the figures closely. What money is coming in and going out of your business? If you can start this habit from the start to monitor cash flow it will be a lot easier for you. It's easy for money to run away from you because you haven't been keeping an eye on where it is going. Be aware of what and where expenditure is going and check there aren't any rogue payments going out as well. Keeping track can be insightful and will help you not only to plan ahead for big expenses, you'll also be able to see where those little sums of money go. On their own smaller amounts of money don't add up to much, but become larger amounts over a period of time. You can do this with your personal finances too.

> **The sooner you have control over**
>
> **your finances the better.**

My husband loves his games and he says it helps him to relax, but when he goes online there are offers and add-ons, which he likes to have. The costs are not necessarily large amounts, usually under £25 at the most, but they add up. I asked if he knew how much he was actually spending each month. In his head, it was a very small amount because those little sums were easily forgotten. He didn't know how much it all totted up to over the course of the month. If it starts to become too high, he needs a reminder to be careful.

It's the same with business. Are there unnecessary regular expenditures which can be cut back or monitored more closely? The sooner you have control over your finances the better it will be for you and your business. When you learn to keep an eye on and manage smaller sums you'll easily be able to do it with larger sums of money too. People with poor money management skills will have money problems no matter how much cash they have.

I did a brilliant course called The Penny Drops: How Money Really Works with Karen Sutton-Johal and Jo Singh Sutton-Johal. In the course they addressed the point; why people don't know how to manage money effectively. It's a lot more complex than not having enough cash flow. Poor spending choices happen for a reason. Karen's book The 4 Money Mindsets explains more.

Don't side step price increases

Price increases can be a prickly and awkward subject for some people, but did you ever believe you were valued in a job where you were never given a pay rise?

Remember your running costs will increase each year even if you don't notice it. It's easy to think more money is coming in, but behind an increase in revenue, there are still all the payments you have to make in order for your business work which also increased in price. You should aim to increase the cost of the services you provide each year. 4 to 10% should be manageable. Thoughtfully planned and communicated you should be able to maintain customer happiness, but regular price increases also stop your product from becoming the cheap option, which is what will happen if you never increase your prices.

> **Your price increase will reflect your growing expertise, experience, and knowledge.**

In a mentoring group, some information was shared from a business manual, which showed if you don't increase your prices, to produce the same profit you would have to increase your sales volume. Increasing your prices will mean your profits will grow and you could still decrease your sales volume to produce the same profit. The point it makes is people are less worried about price than you think and for a business to function smartly you have to increase costs.

Price increases reflect your increasing costs to buy the products you need for your business, insurances, bills, and other overheads. Ultimately your price increase will reflect your growing expertise, experience, and knowledge.

To start you may be more cautious with your price increases and it could be a lower percentage because you're not so confident or comfortable with a bigger one. However, if you don't increase your prices on a regular basis, it will become harder to do the longer you leave it. Be unafraid of increasing your prices from the start and let people know what is going to happen. Never apologise or make excuses to yourself or anyone else for a price increase. Supermarkets and shops don't apologise for putting prices up and people still buy! You're increasing your prices and politely informing everyone concerned as well as thanking them for their continued support and custom.

A price increase in some businesses may be an opportunity to do an offer such as a deal on prepaid appointments for instance. Some people like paying in advance and it means they are more open to having additional services through the year because they have already paid. If you consistently do this every year or 6 months depending on your business model your customers should expect it and as long as you look after their needs, they will stay with you.

It's when the unexpected happens with changes in legislation or other aspects out of your control which you may need to include additional costs. With Covid-19 the time needed to put in extra safety measures and purchase additional PPE equipment required meant increased overheads for many businesses. Now some businesses refused to pass on the cost, but the situation was indefinite. No one knew when the need for extra precautionary measures would stop. The loss of income from shut down was significant already, but to then shoulder on top of it further costs is a lot for any business to bear and to give the same level of service. Something has to give.

Keep track of the controllable activities.

You can either decrease your service by taking something away from it or do a temporary increase due to exceptional circumstances. You may not be comfortable passing on the full cost, but you have to show some sort of increase. A lot of holiday companies will have surcharges because the price of fuel increases or decreases and the resulting fluctuations will impact on fares especially if it's an increase.

When I worked out the time between appointments, extra cleaning, and protective wear it does add up and have a significant impact. In the end, a small surcharge was added to each appointment to show there was a cost there, but it wasn't permanent and only a temporary measure.

Most people accepted this and were understanding of the situation because they had been kept informed of what was going on through written correspondence. This also encouraged them to sign up for prepaid appointments or buy some products. People taking up the offer for the pre-paid appointments showed their commitment and loyalty to the clinic too, which was reassuring.

Keep track of the controllable activities. Make sure if you have lease agreements for equipment or premises they are up to date. If you have equipment to be serviced plan ahead so it remains compliant at all times. If you have insurance renewals, can you look around for better deals? With your insurance renewals double check them. Are you receiving the same benefits as the previous year, or has anything you thought you were covered for been removed to keep the cost looking the same?

> **Check if any legislative changes are going to impact your industry.**

Make sure there will still be adequate cover. If anything happens annually make sure it is accounted for in your yearly financial plan so you are prepared for it especially when there is a cost attached. Don't forget renewals for web domains either.

Check if any legislative changes are going to impact your industry or area of business. Take advice if you are unsure. If you routinely prepare for the activities you know are going to happen then you'll manage situations a lot easier. There's nothing worse than scratching around trying to find the funds to pay for a bill, or deal with something unexpected when with a bit of preparation and forethought the money could have been ready to hand.

If you sign up for and pay for courses, events, or mentoring prioritise the time for them in your diary. It always surprises me how many people pay for these extras, but never actually attend or complete them! You won't learn or gain anything by not going or doing the work. It's easy to sign up for too many activities and then find you don't have the time to actually complete them. This is why you need to organise your time constructively and carefully. Make sure you spend your cash wisely with these investments to obtain the best benefit from them. Don't be beguiled into bargains or the fear of missing out (FOMO). No matter how good something looks or sounds, if you can't be there or do the learning then it's a waste of money.

I took a lot of courses, in fact, there were too many and it was incredibly overwhelming with so much information to absorb, long days spent travelling and attending the courses, it was very tiring. If I could have laid aside the fear of not knowing, picked up more tips and advice from the right people, done fewer courses, but had a better focus on what was really serving the business the most it may have been better with less of a financial strain as well.

The road you have travelled

It's the positive energy you absorb from being around like-minded people who were hungry for change and to develop and grow themselves and their businesses which I desperately wanted, not only for myself, but for my husband to experience too. He was convinced I was being brainwashed by some sort of cult! Eventually, he did go on a couple of the courses, which gave him insight and increased his learning.

> **Going through difficult times will make you more resilient.**

It's incredible to think, years ago the majority of people walked everywhere. The sphere of experience of the average person was a lot narrower. Now, you can travel anywhere and the 'ways and means' to gain new knowledge and communicate is a lot more fluid. If you were to tot up all the places you have been in relation to your learning journey, your business journey, your life journey, you would be looking back on it all and marvelling how far you have progressed.

It wasn't until 2017, literally 31st December 2017 when I finally left the JOB after 5 years of juggling it with the business part-time. Since then the business has grown. I have learned a great deal about myself and business in the process.

Understanding and knowing more about business is paramount, you begin to see and understand tasks differently. You don't always see those tiny increments and improvements yourself because you can only see yourself in the moment, but if were you look back, you'll realise how far you have come along.

All the training, courses, and the people met through them really helped the business when the Covid-19 pandemic hit because mentally I was much more focused and determined. Also, there were people with businesses who understood how it was to be in the same situation who could offer sympathy, advice, and support. Without the knowledge gained from taking courses and having a mentor, financially the business would have been in a very different position.

There's still a lot of uncertainty, but going through difficult times will make you more resilient and stronger mentally than you ever would have been before.

> **Time is the most precious commodity in your business.**

10: Shrewd People Manage Their Time Effectively

Time management is key for any business and the sooner you learn to organise your time the better it will be for you.

> **Constructive use of your time is key.**

It's not only about the time you spend with people, but it's how you spend your time when you're not with them. Constructive use of your time is key. Time is the most precious commodity in your business and a lot of people waste a lot of time in different ways, shapes and forms. You're so very busy being busy and you're not being very effective with your timekeeping and what you're actually doing.

A clock may stop, but time won't

To keep track of myself in the clinic there is a clock on the wall facing me. It's very easy to lose track of time, but you have to be in control of how you use it as much as possible. Think about the service(s) you provide and the time you give doing each service particularly if you're a very hands-on business or it's a 1-2-1 scenario. You also need to be in control of your time doing group sessions in a room or online. Even if you employ others to do work for you, you need to have the systems and processes in place so your employees can continue with their tasks with minimal input from you and do them efficiently, effectively and within a reasonable time scale. If you are having to micro-manage every task then you're not managing your time or your business well.

A simple way for me to talk about this is to relate it to what I do as a Foot Health Practitioner. In a foot health appointment, there is going to be a standard set of actions you would be completing when providing a normal service for someone. When you start out you may be a bit slower because you're not so experienced using the nippers and procedures are a little bit clunky for you because you haven't quite settled into a routine.

Once you have got more confidence, you're going to work a lot more quickly. You soon realise if you give too much time to each person, you're decreasing your hourly value. If there's too much time between each appointment then you're actually wasting time as usually you're unable to concentrate on another task except to wait for the next person to arrive. Yes, you need to tidy up and prepare for the next person, but with practice, this becomes quicker.

A dance around time

It's better for you, if possible, to keep appointments to a block of time or particular days of the week so you're not wasting time. You need to be in control of your diary and time. There's no point in running your business by seeing one person one day with maybe a day or two off before you see another if those sessions take half an hour or so. Appointments at odd times of the day will break it up and disrupt your time and may mean you can't do other more productive activities for you and your business.

> **Don't be intimidated by a client's demands.**

There will need to be some flexibility and you may make allowances with your time to see someone new, but you need to be strategic about it as well. I always try to keep appointments together on the same days. If it looks like there's going to be one odd appointment on a particular day, I can tell them there's no availability on that date and suggest another one.

You hear about people who have clients who dictate to them when they want to be seen. It's a little dance between you and them. You want them to feel they are seeing you when they want to see you, but really, it's when you want to see them. I've heard of practitioners who are saying they put fake appointments in their diary to give an excuse as to why they can't do a particular time or date. Don't be intimidated by a client's demands.

Some people get in touch demanding appointments with little or no notice because they expect to be seen straight away. Suddenly a pain or problem they have had for ages is now urgent in their mind and they want to see someone now. You can allow them to have an appointment at a time less convenient to you, but you have to decide if it is worth it.

> **Your time is very precious.**

In any business, if you want a particular time to be free then block it out as being unavailable. You do not have to justify why. Say you can't do the timeslot if someone asks for one inconvenient for you. It's not anyone's business to know why. There should be times in your day or days in the week sacred to you for whatever reason or purpose it is. You don't have to work 7 days a week if you don't wish; as your own boss, you decide what days you work. If you don't want to work weekends because you want to spend time with your partner, family, or your friends, then don't.

Give and use your time wisely

Your time is very precious. It's not only about the generation of money through the new custom, it's about good time management and making sure you don't overextend or overstretch yourself by trying to squeeze someone else into your day. Working ridiculously long hours in the long term will eventually seriously impact upon your physical and mental well-being, social life, and relationships.

Make sure in your day you give some time for yourself: take regular breaks, hydrate yourself properly, eat or even take a walk in the fresh air. These activities are going to affect your performance, your concentration, and your energy and this can reflect back onto the people you meet. Even 10-15 minutes of time to yourself can make a difference. If you don't look after yourself there's a point where your body and mind stop functioning properly and this is when you're more likely to make rash, poor decisions or make mistakes even.

Don't let the needs of the people you work with manage your time either. It constantly surprises me of the number of practitioners who give ridiculously long appointments *"to get everything done"* for a disproportionately low price. If you have costed your fees to be within a certain time frame, why would you think it profitable to give significant amounts of extra time to *"finish off"*?

When you cost your service, you should cost in your time as well. It's all about your Income Generating Value (IGV). If you give more time for someone, in effect you decrease your IGV or your time value per hour. The relevance of this point is would you work for someone based on what you yourself earn per hour? How you manage your time affects what you earn. Is the person you are dealing with going to appreciate the additional time you've given?

Those very same practitioners bemoan how they're not appreciated, how people say they cost too much, but they give all this extra time to do the work and can't understand why the people they deal with are not thankful. If you can't do what needs to be done in the time you've allocated to complete it, you stop. You either tell the person you are dealing with they have had all the time you've allocated for them today or tell them before you start the time they have booked with you isn't sufficient to do what needs to be done. They can either be booked in again at an appropriate time sooner rather than later to finish off the work that needs to be done. Or if you have the time to do so they will need to pay for the extra work to be done. Don't be shy in asking for an amount reflecting the extra time you are offering for your services.

Penny Briant in her book *How to create more time for you and live an amazing life: Coaching for women* eloquently makes a good point about value when she shows the cost of different roles and tasks women often undertake in the home as if you were being paid a wage for each one. What you do takes time, but also has a value.

Likewise, with someone new don't give too much extra time at the same cost either. It's easy to give extra time for free on the first appointment because you want the person to be impressed with your work so they will want to use you again. Factor in the cost for the extra time needed to take details as well. You pay yourself a lower hourly rate by giving too much extra time for free and people will expect longer sessions afterwards. They're paying you for a service.

Ask them what is most important to them to be dealt with first then order and prioritise what will be done and explain if you cannot complete it all, they may need to book more time or another appointment to finish off the tasks you didn't have time to complete. By doing this they will have to face up to the fact there is more work than normal that needs doing and will respect you, your time, and services more.

> ## Learn to monitor your time.

If a person doesn't want to pay extra for your time, they are either not your ideal customer, or you're not conveying strongly enough the true value you give through your services. For some people having a longer time between appointments can mean it takes longer to do what needs to be done. If this is the case explain the problem particularly highlighting if you have found it hard to complete all the work on time. Sometimes with appointments of a cyclic nature people who choose a longer time frame between each one may not have much that needs doing, it is their choice, but don't charge them the same as if they came during a normal time-frame because you want to offer an incentive for people to come within a shorter time-scale.

Be upfront and transparent with people because not everyone understands business, what the full cost of running a business is and how much every small detail impacts you even when you're giving a few extra minutes at the end of an appointment. Learn to monitor your time and let people know if you've given them extra time.

If people don't understand there's a value for your work, they're not going to value it. People won't be paying what you are worth if they don't understand what your worth is.

People should be aware there is a cost even if you're offering a free session. There are different views on this. Some advice says you should never give your services or products for free because people will become suspicious there is some sort of catch. Some say people won't value what is given for free and you devalue your services by giving too much away for free. A mentor suggested to a group I was in you can give free sessions out if you want to, but invoice it and show the discount on the invoice so the receiver understands while it was a free session they received it still had a value and a price. For high-value services, you would expect to give more of your time because the value you receive at the end is more.

If you offer services, keep track of how long tasks take within your business to make it easier and quicker for you to price up jobs. Trying to make an estimation as to how long work will take to do could leave you out of pocket if you've miscalculated. There are different apps to help you monitor the time it takes to do different tasks. People are impatient. The quicker you can respond with a realistic quote the better.

Expand your stride

If you go for a walk and take little steps your walk would take longer and within a set amount of time you wouldn't travel very far. Expand your stride and you'll probably move quicker and manage to go farther too. Similarly, moving your business online is a good way to extend your reach and stride not only within your local area, but globally too, although serving people in other time zones may mean adjusting your working hours. It can be a brilliant time saver and for people who need to travel a lot for their business, it can be a big money-maker and saver too. Many businesses were pushed to go online due to the Covid-19 situation.

> **There's a time of day when you are at your most productive, effective, efficient, and working to the best of your ability.**

Some people said it pushed them out of their comfort zone to use online apps, whereas beforehand they put off doing this while they were tied up with the day-to-day running of their businesses. Obviously, when you go online make sure the setup looks professional, do some practice runs to make sure all goes smoothly and you'll be fine. You may even record your content, which you could sell as a course or put into resource areas as a part of paid-for content. You could utilise aspects for other content you offer as well.

Expand Your Stride

It's easy to become stuck doing work in a certain way and when something comes along which disrupts the pattern it's either going to be a good or a bad change. You have to decide what it is going to be and make it work for you.

Listen to your working rhythm

Have you heard some people refer to and talk about the 5 am or the 6 am Club? This is where the very busy entrepreneurs and business owners are up before everyone else to do a few extra hours of work. It can be a very productive time as there are fewer distractions.

I believe you should work the hours to suit you as much as you can and when you work at your best because everybody works to a different rhythm. Some people are night owls while others work at their best in the afternoon. There's a time of day when you are at your most productive, effective, efficient, and working to the best of your ability. You're in the zone and you get more done. You should know and learn what time of day it is for you when the work you do is the best quality so you don't have to make as many corrections. Efficiency and accuracy are important in any business. You don't want to be making costly mistakes because you haven't given yourself sufficient time or your brain isn't functioning at its best.

Are you using your best times of the day? You need to utilise your absolute best times to be doing tasks that make the most for you and your business rather than those which eat up into your time. Sometimes it's too easy to do the simpler less important activity. Your focus and best energy should be on the important tasks first. These will focus on your Key Results Areas (KRAs) and what brings the most revenue to your business. Your KRAs should be measurable to know how successful they are as shown by your Key Performance Indicators (KPIs).The less important ones you should be doing at times of the day when you're not quite as functional or ask someone else to do them for you. You can't give all of your time to do everything. As much as possible use other people. Employ a Virtual Assistant (VA) to do the mundane time-consuming office tasks for you or you'll be bogged down doing everything and nothing.

You've got to be constructive about what you do and this is where your daily, weekly and monthly plans will come into play. Each day, week, and month should be mapped out with room for tweaks and adjustments to make sure you're going to be maximizing the time you have and when you're at your best to do those. Your KRAs will always be the priority. You need to be aware of the time you're spending on tasks especially the ones which use up all your time. Social media can help and contribute to your business, but don't let the time you spend on it become counterproductive or too distracting.

11: Healthy People Manage Their Physical Health

Your health and well-being are absolutely crucial for your business and it's something you must protect. There are different aspects of your health you should consider for you to be in the best physical shape and best mental state.

What way is your health going?

Your health journey will either be a positive or a negative one with your progress going one of two ways. If you're already pursuing a healthy lifestyle the continuance of it is paramount. If you're not and you choose from now on to carry on as you are without making any positive healthy changes in your life, your health will deteriorate. Whether it's now or in the future, you will have problems. The only people who don't or are less likely to be affected by health issues, later on, are either actively seeking to look after their health now and intend to maintain it in the future too.

To have a healthy mind and body you need to keep yourself fit and be active. Perhaps you think you are healthy enough, but if you are doing little or nothing for your health, it is only an illusion. Chances are your body is already in an acidic state and in a state of decay. You don't have to be super-fit, but at the very least be reasonably healthy.

Look at the people you know who in the past drank and ate whatever they pleased, exercised little, and see what they look like now. Do they look the same or do they look older than their years? The choices you have already made have already made an impact on your health.

As your body state becomes more acidic it is more likely you're going to fall prey to illness and disease. What price and value do you actually put on your health? If you can't answer or if you don't value it highly enough then expect to have increasing health issues and problems. You'll invest in something if you feel you have a need and a desire to have it because it will either solve an existing problem or make another aspect of your life easier and better. Many people have come to my clinic because of a problem they have ignored and have not only let it become worse, but painful as well.

> **Poor food or life-style choices create an acidic environment in your body.**

So many people ignore their health. If you don't look after yourself now you will find it harder to enjoy or appreciate fully anything you do when your health fails. Or worse, you won't be able to do the activities you want to. If you're offered the opportunity to take control of your health, the answer more often or not is you can't afford it or you don't have the time. However, you always have the money to spend on things which make your health worse, and you know what they are: whether it's drinking, smoking, meals out, or indulgent treats. Even if it means cutting back a little or forgoing one meal out at a restaurant each month to save an extra bit of money to invest in your health, most people will refuse to do so or to make any sacrifices.

Poor food or life-style choices create an acidic environment in your body. How many of you know and understand this? You only notice when health issues and problems start.

Poor diet caused not only digestive issues, but my skin became inflamed, sore, and irritated, I was constantly tired and lethargic. For a long time, I didn't understand what the real cause was. It was an overload of carbohydrates. Too many fizzy drinks, bad food choices, sugars and sweets, and crazy amounts of them had taken their toll. It all creates stresses on your body, which in turn affects your mood and energy.

Every single one of you is unique and you'll each have your own triggers and weaknesses when it comes to food or drinks. Firstly, you need to admit to what they are before you can begin to address them. If you want a more detailed analysis of your health, you can have tests to find out how imbalanced or out of tune your body is so you can redress those issues.

The sociable businessperson

Food and meals with people may be a part of your business to help build rapport and trust. Maybe you have this routine where you meet potential prospects for a social cup of coffee or some sort of beverage and you have a piece of cake or something to eat with it. You may slot your networking meetings into mealtimes. Weight gain is usually quite subtle and often goes unnoticed. Small weight gains each year amount up until suddenly you realise you have a much larger girth. Managing your networking around events and places where calorie laden less nutritious food is available on a regular basis will not only affect your waistline, but your energy.

I noticed this in particular with all-day training events. There's some food and snacks when you arrive, then a break with more snacks and after lunch another break with more snacks. Before you know where you are you've consumed a considerable amount of food there. You've had a big calorific intake with little or no exercise because you've been seated all day and then drove home to sit down in front of the television. You may enjoy a glass of or two of wine because you need to absorb all the information from the day or to decompress, unwind and relax.

It's not only about weight gain and the repercussions to your health, it's about the effect on your energy and mood also. With less energy you'll find it more difficult to complete tasks. Poor food choices and not enough exercise can affect your sleep patterns and caffeine-laden drinks to help keep you working will exacerbate this further. When you're tired, you're more likely to make poor decisions, be irritable, lethargic, which in turn will make you feel less inclined to go out and do something healthy.

Alcohol at events may make it more social but having too much alcohol can affect your health especially if alcohol becomes a habit. And alcohol is calorie-laden. Social drinking often combines well with social eating. Alcohol is often used as a way to wind down in an evening, but it's easy to lose track of how much you're consuming, and this again can affect your health and sleep patterns.

The impact of poor eating habits

Sometimes working away from home or long hours spent travelling can disrupt your eating habits. If you're busy all day, do you end up eating large heavy meals late at night or binging on sweets and chocolates to keep you going? Irregular mealtimes, skipping meals, and then eating unhealthy convenience foods won't help you either.

On the other hand, if the way your business works means you are at home or in an office it's easy to become absorbed in what you're doing and not to have enough breaks.

I do this sometimes with the clinic and when booking people in I try to book the appointments together on the same day to maximise time, without blocking out time for myself to have a break.

It's easy to fall into a cycle of poor eating habits and possibly poor hydration too because you're so busy.

Wearing a mask all day for the clinic is no fun, but you don't always hydrate enough.

Your body needs to be fuelled with the right foods and nutrition and be properly hydrated to function optimally.

It astounds me how in the UK in particular there are so many obese young adults walking around. How many will make it to significant old age and have a good quality of health? In 2018 from the UK population 67% of men and 60% of women were classed as being overweight or obese.

The results of those poor choices are seen in the clinic. People with significant health issues and problems who are unable to enjoy their life to the fullest. People expect medical science will solve their problems and take an increasing myriad of pills, potions, lotions and creams for a growing list of health issues. Younger people will be needing more and more assistance if they don't take control of their well-being.

> **The best choice for your health is to be the healthiest version of yourself.**

Prescribed medicines are not necessarily the best option for your overall health in the long term. A growing and worrying trend are situations where people are having to take pills to counter the effects of other medicines they are taking. The best choice for your health is to be the healthiest version of yourself.

It's not complicated. Keep your brain and body active. Drink plenty of clean water, take a varied amount of exercise and eat healthy food. *Mary Morris and Rosemary Conley's 28 Day Immunity Plan* offers sound advice, meal plans, and exercises which can easily be slotted into your daily routine. Too often people don't even know what a healthy diet is despite all the information available, and don't understand how much exercise is needed or worse don't want to be bothered because it's too much effort. It's easy for you to wear clothing in a larger size, to buy and eat a quick convenience meal, to switch on the TV and slump in front of it or play mindlessly with distracting gadgets and gizmos.

The healthiest people eat, drink and exercise in moderation. They're not depriving themselves. They are mentally and physically active and have good healthy social interactions. The people who have a vibrant and active social life, go out and interact with others are more well-adjusted and happier even if they do still have health issues.

The people who don't find their health suffers while their life becomes very stagnant with little or no stimulation and social interaction. With failing health can come failing health standards, less energy, and for some personal hygiene deteriorates as well. Depression, anxiety, and isolation set in, which can be very debilitating and can perpetuate a negative outlook. The less physically active you are the more difficult it will be to put yourself out there and it becomes a vicious circle.

Your future health vision

The steps you are taking now towards your health will lead you to your future self. If you've got too comfortable and complacent with where you are now and it's too much effort to change, envision if you will, your future self and base it on how you are now.

- What do you look like?
- What are you doing all day?

> **Fitter people are often able to manage illnesses, stress, and pain a lot easier than unfit people.**

It's the life you live in now but amplified. If you sit around doing little exercise now, then your future self will be doing the same. If you are overweight, your future self will be bigger. If you feel your life is boring now, what life will your future self be leading? If you are starting to have health issues now, your future self will have even worse issues to deal with.

But now visualize your future self as a healthy person. What are you doing? Who are you with? How do you feel, how do you look? What are you wearing even?

Which version of you would you rather be? Your healthier and hopefully happier self? Or the amplified version of yourself today who is unhealthy, unhappy, and dissatisfied?

Even if you don't feel you have any health issues it may be you are finding it harder to maintain your weight or your weight is creeping up even though you don't think you are doing anything different. If you have this lethargy about you, imagine it amplified. You may have heard the older you are the more difficult it is to be fit and healthy and part of the reason for this is any habits and thoughts you have now will be even more firmly entrenched when you're older.

Fitter people often manage illnesses, stress, and pain a lot easier than unfit people and find it less stressful too.

Make time for your health

How can you manage your health better? If you need to, plan something. Put exercise in as a part of your daily or weekly routine, as you plan your business plan do the same with your health. Have the end result in mind; of what you want to achieve. What time and days will you put aside for exercise? Sometimes exercise feels like the hard option especially when you're not feeling too good. You tell yourself you'll leave it till next time. If you make excuses such as you don't have the time or you're not a sporty person then you will always give yourself reasons not to exercise. Perhaps you think to be fit, you have to do some sort of sport? You don't have to be a sporty person but you do need to find the physical activity to suit you and your personality and the time you have. Don't ever force yourself to do something you don't enjoy.

If you refuse to take responsibility for yourself or make excuses, then you will stagnate.

I try to exercise every day if only for 15 to 20 minutes.

Exercises help to strengthen you mentally and physically. Do you want to end up in a physical state where you can't do simple activities? As you age you want to keep yourself as strong and fit as you can. If you allow your strength to go you lose your independence and you'll be relying on other people. Those people can't be there for you all the time.

A friend of mine has got considerably weaker in her hands because she does so little physically.

If you don't engage the muscles in your body and you lead a sedimentary lifestyle with little exercise, then your body will become weaker. Exercise doesn't only stimulate the body; it helps your cognitive state too.

The self-isolation rules of Covid-19 saw a massive deterioration in the physical and mental health of a lot of older people, while younger people had greater anxiety. How many of you take yourself out of your everyday environment to move around a bit more and to look at something different? How well are you really?

You have to push yourself because the people who push themselves accomplish the most and gain more satisfaction because they have achieved their goals. Don't make a health goal too difficult to achieve either or you'll become disheartened and dissatisfied and go back to your old ways. Keep a record of how you were at the start to give yourself a way to measure how much you have transformed. You can record your weight, although you ideally only need to weigh yourself once a week. Don't let the number on the scales obsess you because if you're exercising the right way you should be gaining muscle which is heavier than fat. Do a checklist and photos of you at the start of your wellness journey to record how you look and feel and what your measurements are. Keeping bodily measurements can be more satisfying because you'll see the change in body shape as the body gains more muscle definition.

Understanding the Tables

These simple tables will give you a place to start. Update these on a weekly or monthly basis to track and chart your process.

Meals (Week 1)				
	Every Day	**Most days (4-6 days)**	**Some days (1-3 days)**	**Rarely/ Never**
Do you have breakfast?				
Do you have lunch?				
Do you have an evening meal?				
Do you have a mid-morning snack?				
Do you have a late evening snack?				
Notes				

Table 1

The times of day where you succumb to bad snacks or find yourself overindulging should be addressed as this will affect your overall mood as well (see Table 1).

Some scales tell you the percentage of body fat and other details so you can record those too (see Table 3).

The reason for recording your mood and concentration is because it may highlight times of the day when your energy levels are dipping and you'll be more vulnerable to making bad food choices as well as poor decisions for you and your business (see Table 4).

Body Measurement (always measure at the widest point)												
Week	1	2	3	4	5	6	7	8	9	10	11	12
Neck												
Chest												
Waist												
Hips												
Top Thigh												
Top Arms												
Notes												

Table 2

Weight (always weigh yourself on the same day and time of the week)												
Week	1	2	3	4	5	6	7	8	9	10	11	12
Weight												
Notes												

Table 3

Mood and Concentration	Week 1	Week 2
Do you have regular meal times?		
Do you find you energy dips during the morning? If so at what time?		
Do you find your energy dips during the afternoon? If so at what time?		
Do you find your energy levels are low during the evening?		
What are your mood and concentration levels like during the morning?		
What are your mood and concentration levels like during the afternoon?		
What are your mood and concentration levels like during the evening?		
Do you have rest days either at the weekend or during the week?		
What are your energy and mood levels like on your rest days?		
Do you have time for interests and hobbies outside of your work?		
Notes		

Table 4

What days of the week do you exercise and how long?							
Week	M	Tu	W	Th	F	Sa	Su
1							
2							
3							
4							
5							
6							
7							
8							
9							
10							
11							
12							

Notes

Table 5

Meals (Week 12)				
	Every Day	Most days (4-6 days)	Some days (1-3 days)	Rarely/ Never
Do you have breakfast?				
Do you have lunch?				
Do you have an evening meal?				
Do you have a mid-morning snack?				
Do you have a late evening snack?				
Notes				

Table 6

If you have started to follow a healthy eating plan you should see a significant improvement in your eating and snacking habits in particular. Compare your answers on Table 1 and Table 6.

> **Your good intentions can often fall by the wayside if you do not have anyone to stay accountable to.**

By honestly filling in these tables, you should be able to see patterns of behaviour you can address and change or recognise where there are areas in your health and well-being you need to work on. If you follow a plan to improve your health and fitness by keeping a record at the start you will be able to measure your progress and improvement. The more detail of your own you add the more you will gain from this exercise.

If you have someone to offer support, you're more likely to achieve your aim. Your good intentions can often fall by the wayside if you do not have anyone to be accountable to.

Your health is your wealth

It's really important to look after yourself. I've been to Continuing Professional Development (CPD) events where professionals and practitioners there are not in the best state of health themselves. You can see it simply by looking at them. They've got dark circles under their eyes and their skin looks pasty. They're overweight because they're not giving time for themselves, to take exercise or to eat nutritionally balanced meals.

The irony is the events I'm at these are people whose businesses will be health-related and the people they serve will be coming to see them to have help with their health needs! As a practitioner, if you have clients with health issues and you're trying to guide them to look after their health better, but you yourself are not in the best state of health will it inspire them to change?

Your health matters if your business relies solely on you. Consider this. If you fall ill, can you work? Maybe you would battle through if it was a little cold, but if you deal with vulnerable people would you want to put their health at risk? If you keep succumbing to every bug out there it is a sign your body is struggling, each time it will sap your energy and be harder to recover.

There comes a time when you need to make yourself well again. If you've been working way too many hours, if you've not been watching what you eat, how you look after your nutrition, your exercise, and you're run down you're going to have no energy and your immune system will be weaker.

When you fall ill your body is giving you a message. You need to take a break. You need to become well again and this is going to cost you, particularly if you have to cancel appointments due to illness. But if you don't let yourself recover properly the long-term damage to your health could take a long time to repair.

Even the weather can affect your mood and overall aspect. Give yourself some time outside in natural daylight. Seasonal Affective Disorder (SAD) can particularly affect some people in the winter months due to less hours of daylight. If you're stuck indoors all day, buy a light to help with this.

Even the room and environment you work in matters. Some people find an air-conditioned room dries the skin and can make it sore and irritated, while a stuffy room can leave you feeling tired and lethargic. What can you change to make it better for you? The place where you relax and unwind at the end of the day matters also. A cluttered and dirty environment is bad for your mental and physical health too. If you can't make the time to keep it clean and tidy find a cleaner to help.

12: Healthy People Manage Their Mental Health

How you think can be one of your greatest assets when running a business. It's what drives you to get up in the morning. It helps you to step out of your comfort zone, take actions which aren't easy and make those difficult decisions.

> **Everything you think, say and do**
>
> **has a resulting action.**

Consider your mental state. How do you start your day? What intentions do you set yourself and put out there before you actually begin working? What you think, what you say, how you act and respond to any given situation will define you; everything you think, say, and do has a resulting action.

Everyone has a different viewpoint

Here's the equation. The event (what happened) minus the response or reaction (what did you do, how did you feel?) equals the outcome (what was the result?). How you behave and the reaction and responses you give can be either positive or negative.

Trivial and minor events shouldn't affect you or be allowed to be blown out of proportion. People and situations may trigger you, but they don't need to define you.

Mental Health

Every day in the hated job and supposedly as part of a particular team, I walked into the office and said, "Good morning!" Nine times out of ten it was ignored and fed up with the negative responses decided to ignore them back only to be told it had been noted I wasn't saying good morning. It left me with conflicted emotions about going into a room full of people. Not knowing how it will go, how anyone will react, what will happen, makes it stressful, but then no one else knows either.

Your life experiences will influence your view and your responses, while every person's reaction to each and every situation and scenario they are presented with will vary. Some of you will love going to new places, going out to meet new people, speaking to them and it's really exciting for you. Some of you may worry about receiving negative responses, being in different settings or may be uncomfortable being around people you are unfamiliar with.

Past events and your memories of them embed themselves into your mind, but those events are as far away from the reality you're now in as you can imagine. It's not always about you. How people behave, respond or react to you could be because they're having a bad day; they could have argued with their partner; the kids were playing up this morning; they had a bad journey travelling; maybe they had some bad news or are worried about something. You try to process it in your mind. Do you blame yourself? Do you get upset? You don't know what's going on in someone else's life, but behind it all there's a human being.

> **In any situation, there's an opposite reaction, thought or idea you can adopt.**

You'll meet and encounter people who think about themselves and don't care or know how what they say or do negatively impacts on others. Even when you're in a situation where it makes you uncomfortable or upset, you don't have to accept it, but you don't need to let it negatively affect you either. Sometimes it's better to let those emotions blow over, take a deep breath and think through your response. In the *Instant Switch, Sandy Gilad* suggests you ask yourself, *"What is another way I can think about this?"* It's quite a journey of self-discovery, but the truth is in any situation there's an opposite reaction, thought or idea you can adopt.

It's natural to try and rationalise the responses you receive. Some people won't notice or be bothered because it doesn't matter to them and they are focused on themselves only. Others will notice but are confident enough in themselves to deal with it and won't take it personally. Then there will be those who do notice, take it personally and become upset, then either become confrontational or critical or retreat into themselves because they think they have done something wrong and blame themselves.

By transferring poor responses and reactions from previous events onto other people, you put a negative energy where it does not belong. Stop the negative dialogue and the criticism with yourself.

Change your intention

How do you break out of this? How do you stop yourself from being dropped into other people's negative responses in any situation? It's better to take some positive energy and bring positive energy to a room than to bring negative energy into a room or to take it away with you. Sometimes you have to stop yourself from taking it further or the emotions can become out of control. You need to tell yourself you're okay and leave it there.

Have you ever been anywhere where a person who in some way or other made an impact on your day? The tasks they performed could have been as banal as directing you into a parking space or the room where you were going for some sort of seminar for instance. Doesn't it make a difference when someone is personable, they're interacting with you in a way which shows they're enjoying it?

Now, imagine the difference when you meet a person who isn't interested, who doesn't want to help, and really doesn't want to be there. They are there for the pay and can't wait to leave and go home. It's a very different experience, isn't it? Their sour mood affects you and your energy dips. *Lisa Davies* talks beautifully about doing even the smallest things with gratitude in her book *Get a Life – The Guide Book.*

No matter who you are or what you do, the way you set your intentions will impact not only on your day, but also on the people you meet. In business, you want to put the best version of you out there. Every person will have a different approach. It could be visualisation exercises or meditation or your morning routine, but whatever it is, it sets you up for the day ahead with a more focused and positive mind.

> **People who give themselves time to prepare and focus achieve better results.**

Basically, in some way shape or form with visualisation, you're imagining or seeing in your mind the best version of something. You could be focusing on your business and what you want for it. You could be thinking about the day ahead of you for instance and how it's going to be. Whether you do this first thing in the morning or last thing at night, do it when it best suits you and when you feel it's most productive. You will need to be in a relaxed state with no disturbances.

The point of visualisation is you are imagining the very best version of what it is you want to happen. Visualise every aspect and detail of it from how you interact with people, what you say, what you do, how you react, what you hear and what you see etc.

Visualisation Board

You could state your intention for the day ahead. Some people have particular words or phrases they repeat on a daily basis to themselves or out loud while they visualize something about how the day ahead will be. Maybe you like to play a particular type of music or song while you do this. I use affirmations with the essential oils I use on a daily basis. You could write your intention down in a diary or journal. It could be you listen to a relevant podcast or mindset audio to set you up for your day. Going for a run or a walk or doing some form of exercise may help you to gain clarity and focus. Exercise such as yoga and meditation are all really good because it clears your mind and helps focus you on the present.

People who give themselves time to prepare and focus achieve better results. If you aren't giving yourself the time you need to prepare chances are your life is going to be chaotic and disorganized with haphazard results. If your life has no structure and your day is poorly planned or organised, you will be less focused on the right things and reacting more to events as they happen.

When you go to places for meetings, give yourself time to be in the right mood. When you're not prepared your day goes from one task to the next, you're either late, flustered, disorganised or forgetting important points and you have less control. Don't be the busy person, doing nothing and getting nowhere in the process. You don't have to be super organised, but you do need to be on top of things and come across as being professional and prepared mentally.

An untidy environment can affect your well-being and health, but it could reflect a very cluttered mind and on a practical level, it can be more difficult to find items. It's about looking after what you have.

Move to a positive state of thinking

A positive frame of mind can be a really potent asset because in business there may be setbacks or problems and you need to have the mental resilience to deal with them. The more positive your way of thinking is the more likely it is you're going to overcome problems quicker than people with a more negative view of life.

> **A prepared and positive mind**
>
> **is a focused mind.**

For some, if there's a problem it quickly becomes a state of overwhelm and they give up instead of trying to think more creatively on how to solve them. If your life is in a constant state of chaos and disorganisation it's harder to find focus. A prepared and positive mind is a focused mind.

How do you reset those tightly ingrained patterns of self-belief? You have to believe you can do so for a start. You have to stop being reliant on other people for everything and remove yourself from the cycle of blame. It's easy to blame others when your meeting or your day does not go well, but every action has its cause and effect. You can't be in control of everything which happens to you, but you can decide to change how you think about it.

- How resilient are you?
- Do you resist change or are you the change?
- How far will you go to find different and alternative activities?

If you have a problem, how do you solve it? Or do you hope it will go away and sort itself out? You have to keep moving forward and planning towards your future. Setbacks happen even to the most successful people. The difference is successful people focus on what works or they fix or improve whatever is not working so well but are still relevant and beneficial to their needs. More importantly, they don't allow themselves to be bogged down with unnecessary distractions.

Are you in a negativity loop right now? It's easy for you to tell yourself you can't, but why don't you change the dialogue? Tell yourself you can.

Consider all the things once deemed impossible. And yet now they are commonplace; they are possible. Do you dare to dream of better and to believe you can have more? Some of the most unlikely people have been successful in areas no one ever thought they could. They've overcome adversity, difficulties, and struggles simply because they used their imagination, belief, and vision to make the dreams they wanted a reality.

How you think and your mindset is moulded in you from a young age. Most children want to go everywhere and explore; then they're told not to. You're told you should conform, fit in and follow the crowd. Is this you? If you fly in the other direction there's a chance you may find different answers, opportunities, and experiences. See the possibilities, not the impossibilities. A friend of mine, Elaine Godley, survived her cancer and she discusses her cancer journey in her book. She didn't accept conventional treatments. She's always seeking new answers and approaches to her health which are holistic and more in tune with her body. Following a conventional approach means you'll never find the alternatives.

Do you ever think about how you love and care for yourself? How you respond and react can be because of your need to be loved, but firstly you need to love yourself because to give or receive love in every aspect cannot happen if you don't put yourself and your needs first. You can't love yourself either if you're always putting yourself into situations or allowing yourself to be in a situation where it is causing you to be harmed whether physically or mentally. What dialogues do you have with your inner self? What do you say to yourself? Listen to the dialogue you play to yourself. Are there signs showing that all is not right? What you say to yourself today is the repetition of what you've said to yourself yesterday and each day before. If it is a negative dialogue, then what does it say about how you think about yourself?

It's like when you drive a car. Anyone who drives will know you actually don't think about a lot of the actions you take as you drive. You don't have to stop to think about how you're going to change gears; you do it automatically. If you're taking the same route, chances are you don't even think about it when you change lane; once more you do it automatically.

It's the same with negative thought processes. Do you ever stop yourself or pause and take note? If you actually analyse what you say or think to yourself, you may notice those little dialogues you keep having with yourself are affecting the way you think and feel about yourself and your life in general.

Look at what the outcomes are every time you're feeling negative, down, upset, angry, moody, hurt, or whatever it is, if it's the same then you've got to start changing your responses and start treating yourself differently. Stop, acknowledge it, work it through, and then rationalize it. You can't always control what happens, but you can control your response because your response can either make your mood worse or better.

With numerous thoughts going through your head each and every day, you may find yourself unexpectedly dwelling on the past. It doesn't have to be your distant past. It could be something from the day before upset you; you've dwelled on it, you're remembering it, you're still ruminating on the past moment and you don't get over it. Is it a very loving way to treat yourself? Even if you're dwelling on positive memories, you're still not living in your here and now. Memories can put you in a positive state but can also deflect your energy from building a happier more prosperous future.

When you love yourself, you will find it easier to forgive what's happened in the past and any past mistakes you and others have made which have affected you. Whatever has happened whether or not it was your fault if you treat yourself in a negative and unloving way it means you cannot own it or take responsibility for your actions and what you say or do. If you're always playing the blame game, you're never moving forward. To forgive is one of the most healing and empowering choices you can make for yourself and I admire people who truly do this.

Or maybe you think of your future? Dreaming of a better future is no good if you take no steps or action today to make it a reality.

There may be times when you doubt yourself, but if you doubt yourself who will believe you? Believe you can, and you will. If you never believed you could be anything chances are you've never tried. Don't rely on what other people think of you either. Self-belief comes from within. You're not always going to receive praise in your life.

Present the best version of yourself

It can be very damaging not only for your mental outlook, but for your reputation if you are constantly finding a negative viewpoint. Look at your social media. Get rid of the negativity in there. A simple way to address this, if it's online, is read back your initial response before pressing send. There's many a time when I have read and then deleted what was written. It's easy to respond in the moment and to regret it after.

I started doing a post every Monday with the hashtag #mondaysmile on LinkedIn to share a message about what you can do to uplift yourself and others. Changing how you think is very powerful and you can change your thoughts to more positive ones and vice versa. It's nice to receive feedback from people who have enjoyed the posts and found the content useful too.

Being helpful and giving good advice goes a long way to build a connection and trust with people. Be genuine and put forward the best version of yourself as much as you can and you will reap the rewards.

You can't always solve a problem
yourself; you need help.

Epilogue: The Big Leap

Has a fear ever stopped you from taking action? Whether or not you recognize it as fear is it logical? Most of the time, no. You tell yourself a lot of untruths. There will be thoughts and decisions you struggle with, but with practice and determination you can overcome, and you will surprise yourself with what you can do.

You may have wondered why this book is called *Step On That Corn*. It's a foot joke essentially and many people come to the clinic because they have a problem with their feet. It's the pain point. You can't always solve a problem yourself; you need help. Corns are often painful, but you have to step out of your comfort zone and arrange to see someone who can help you to resolve the issue. When a person puts their foot on the ground after a corn has been dealt with the expression of relief on their face and the gratitude is immense. It's only a small lump on their foot, but it caused so much bother. Starting a business is the same. There are going to be some painful parts, but once you've got through them, you'll feel so much better.

As a little girl my parents would take the family on a holiday and every other year we went abroad. My favourite and most memorable holiday was to beautiful Italy. I remember it so vividly, the big huge slices of juicy watermelon served after our supper, on a rainy day when I wanted to go in the hotel pool, the go-karting, the boat trip out in the evening to a little restaurant to eat grilled fish and the way the lights

The Big Leap

danced on the water in the darkness. There were so many wonderful memories and experiences.

But one memory stands out. We went out for the day and were at this pool, which had three diving boards. There were lots of people there. Adults lulling by the pool and kids splashing about in the warm water, while the older kids were diving into the pool. The little baby diving board was easy to jump off and felt safe. The next one was a bit higher and gave a little rush off excitement when jumping off it, but it still felt safe. There was me, a little girl around 8 years old in her swimsuit, with some other kids jumping off the second board, climbing out of the pool to go back up to jump off it again while laughing and giggling and having fun.

In the excitement, I started climbing up to the third and highest, which was on a platform.

At first, it felt OK, but going higher the sounds of the people chattering got less noisy and there was a moment of hesitation, to go back, but during this pause for thought, some young lads started to climb up. They were lean Italians with tans, dark hair and there was a look in their dark eyes. Being a little girl, it was way scarier to try and go back down past them as they were several years older.

I carried on, but I was starting to feel scared as it was so high up. The lads at the top were impatiently waiting their turn and one by one they jumped off the platform into the blue water of the pool below. I was beginning to feel really nervous and scared because it was so high up but looking at the growing line of young lads all glaring at me with those dark eyes it was impossible to turn back. A little boy of similar age to me clambered past to go back down, too ashamed to look anyone in the eye.

Suddenly the platform was clear and I was next. With quivering legs, I slowly moved towards the edge of the platform. It was giddily high. If you've ever seen cartoons as a child, you may have seen ones where a pool and a very high diving board were involved. The big huge pool turns into the tiniest most shallow paddling pool, while the diving board at the top morphs into the tiniest most flimsy-looking board. The other characters are tanned, muscular, and lean with angular chins and super white teeth and do the most perfect dives and somersaults as they go down. Sometimes it's so high, there are bored-looking birds flying past and the odd fluffy cloud floating by.

Those cartoons convey a truth because from the top of a high diving board the pool does look like it's miles away. I tentatively moved towards the edge. A final look at the lads behind me and the looks on their faces seemed to say don't you dare come back down. With no familiar face to reassure or encourage or offer support, you realise you're on your own and you've got to do something.

There was nowhere else to go, so I jumped and a load of new thoughts came to mind. No one wants to do a belly flop from this height. I kept my arms crossed across my chest, legs straight and toes pointed, and eyes and mouth firmly shut. Going down, I could feel the air across my skin, but suddenly there was a loud splash. In the water you don't stop, your momentum means you keep going downwards and a new terror comes to mind, "You'll drown if you don't swim to the surface."

All around the sounds of the people chatting and laughing by the pool were muffled by the water. Instinct steps in. I came to my senses and frantically started to paddle my arms and move my legs in a bid to make it back up to the surface. After what felt like ages my head broke through the water and I took a gulp of air and felt incredible relief. Then there was the scramble to move to the edge of the pool *because I thought the next diver would land on top of my head else.*

The point is after all the drama, there was no great applause or congratulations. No big cheer went up. My parents hadn't even noticed this monumental jump had been made by their daughter.

> **Little wins and achievements**
>
> **will be amazing to you.**

Business is like this too. There isn't going to be someone cheering you on at every step of the way or congratulating you on all you do. Little wins and achievements will be amazing to you, but to someone else, they won't mean anything. They'll be challenges you'll face and you'll take actions which scare you or take you out of your comfort zone. You'll have to work out the solutions yourself. Some decisions will be easy; some will be hard.

Embrace the adventure

Every day should feel like an adventure for you. You should be educating yourself and moving yourself forward. You're very lucky to be alive. You are a Survivor whether or not you think it. If you're not how you want to be mentally or physically and you're not in the place you want to be, you can still make changes to your situation. Look at all the positives in yourself and the fact you've made it this far. What other people think doesn't matter so much. Every day is a transformation, but you don't see it in yourself. The process takes time.

Some of the most successful people started their businesses later on in their lives and it could have been after years of neglecting themselves through poor decisions, actions, and choices. Eventually, a wake-up call will pushed them to make a decision to change their life. It takes mental maturity and clarity to happen. Your time will come when you're ready to take action and start to make those changes.

It is about taking little steps to start with in business. For every person, those steps will be different based on your experience. As you grow in confidence and start to notice positive results it will give you the impetus to continue. Sometimes, you'll think you're not getting anywhere, but if you keep a record, you will see you've achieved more than you thought you ever could.

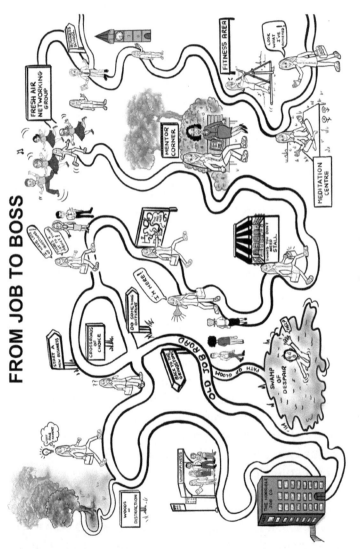

MAP - Journey from Job to Boss

Acknowledgements

Anthony, my hubby, for helping to get the webpage out there. Reminding me to rest up and telling me not to feel bad for taking a break from the business even though I had 101+ things to do!

Ana, my trusted VA. Your guinea pig pictures cheer me up any day.

The Cats, I don't think you helped at all, but you were always there in your own indifferent and disinterested cat way.

Chris at Wittypics, for her fabulous illustrations, which just add some fun and humour to the book.

Ladey, having someone there to mentor me through the process of writing this book was a great help and motivator.

David Balen, Punit Bhatia, Penny Briant, Tony Brown, Roger Cheetham, Lisa Davies, John Falkner-Heylings, Elaine Godley, Sharon Griffiths, Julie Hogbin, Kerry Malster, Hayley Meakes, Gija Melnupe, Nicola O'Brian, Nicola Rose, Karen Sutton-Johal, Johanna Thompson and **Suzie Welstead** for your kind words and endorsements.

Family, friends, my wonderful clinic customers and business associates.

Finally, a big thank you to **everyone** who has shown interest and support in this book.

Glossary

Word or Acronym	Meaning
App	An application, especially as downloaded by a user to a mobile device.
B2B	Business-to-business.
B2C	Business-to-customer.
Blog	Is a truncation of the words web log and features an informal website sharing discussions and information in reverse chronological order so the most recent item is at the top.
CPD	Continuing Professional Development is a way of maintaining and developing your learning and growth beyond your initial training.
Data Protection	Sometimes referred to as data security or information, this relates to the ways you can secure the privacy, availability, and integrity of your information and data.
DISC	Disc profiling refers to the 4 main behavioural styles. D stands for Dominance, I stands for Influence, S stands for Steadiness, and C stands for Conscientiousness.

Word or Acronym	Meaning
E-business card	Electronic business card.
FHP	Foot Health Practitioner.
FOMO	Fear of Missing Out.
GDPR	The General Data Protection Regulation is a legal framework with strict guidelines for the collection and processing of personal information from individuals living in the European Union.
HMRC	Her Majesty's Revenue and Customs.
IGT	Income Generating Tasks.
IGV	Income Generating Value.
JOB	According to the acronym finder there's 18 meanings, but the one I know and was introduced to by someone on a course was JUST OVER the BREADLINE or JUST OVER BROKE. The inference being that in a JOB you're just about managing to get by. https://www.acronymfinder.com/JOB.html.
KPI	Key Performance Indicator.
KRA	Key Result Area.
MLM	Multi-Level Marketing also known as network marketing where people recruit people into the business to sell products or services. (Not to be confused with Pyramid schemes which are illegal!).

Word or Acronym	Meaning
NFC Tag	Near Field Communication tag reader technology allows users to make secure transactions, exchange digital content, and connect electronic devices with a touch. It can also connect with wireless devices.
NHS	National Health Service.
Overhead	Cost or expense.
PAYE	PAYE - or 'pay as you earn' - refers to income tax which is deducted from your salary.
People remember how things made them feel	Buehner was quoted as saying, *"They may forget what you said — but they will never forget how you made them feel."* In Richard Evans' Quote Book, a 1971 compilation of quotations of prominent figures in the LDS church. This quote is often misattributed to many others including Maya Angelou. https://en.wikipedia.org/wiki/Carl_W._Buehner.
PPE	Personal Protective Equipment.
QR Code	Quick Response code which when scanned gives access information instantly.
Reflexology	Is a type of massage where different amounts of pressure are applied to the feet, hands, and ears and uses a theory that these body parts are connected to certain organs and body systems.
ROI	Return on Investment.
SAD	Seasonal Affective Disorder.

Word or Acronym	Meaning
SMART	Specific, Measurable, Assignable, Realistic, Time-Related.
SMARTER	An extension of Doran's S.M.A.R.T. goals (although I don't know who first made the addition to it) with the E being Evaluate and R being Readjust.
STRUCTURE	System, Target, Relevant, Understand, Communicate, Time, Understood, Review, Evaluate.
VA	Virtual Assistant is a person who provides remote administrative support.
VLOG	A vlog is a video log version of a blog and often combines embedded video (or a video link) with supporting text, images, and other meta data.

References

Introduction:

Websites

Facts about women in business, Prowess women in business, https://www.prowess.org.uk/facts, 11/08/2021

The 19 best business books for women (to read in 2021), Upjourney, Carmen Jacob, https://upjourney.com/best-business-books-for-women, 11/08/2021

64% of Britain's Workforce Wants To Set Up Their Own Business, SME loans, Lis Rosling, https://smeloans.co.uk/blog/64-percent-of-britains-workforce-want-to-start-a-business/, 18/03/21

Frequently Requested Stats, fundsquire, Alex Kepka, https://fundsquire.co.uk/startup-statistics/, 11/8/21

Chapter 1: Perceptive People Know Change Will Be Better

Book

Sinek, Simon, Start With Why, (Penguin), 2011

Chapter 2: Enlightened People Are Attracted To The Right Business

Websites

14 Free Personality Tests That'll Help You Figure Yourself Out, The Muse, Alyse Kalish, https://www.themuse.com/advice/14-free-personality-tests-thatll-help-you-figure-yourself-out, 19/03/21

Behavioural Psychology, DISC profiling by Elaine Godley, Elaine Godley, https://www.discprofilingbyelainegodley.com/, 19/03/21

How important is education for business owners and entrepreneurs?, smallbusiness.co.uk, Stefano Maifreni, https://smallbusiness.co.uk/how-important-is-education-for-business-owners-and-entrepreneurs-2473157/, 19/03/21

Transform Great Potential Into Greater Performance, Gallup, Editorial, https://www.gallup.com/cliftonstrengths/en/252137/home.aspx, 19/03/21

What is Continuing Professional Development (CPD)?, Jobs. ac.uk, Lucie Johnston, https://career-advice.jobs.ac.uk/career-development/what-is-continuing-professional-development-cpd/, 16/09/21

Chapter 3: A Curious Person Starts With Questions

Books

Bhatia, Punit, Intro to GDPR: A Plain English Guide to Compliance, (Advisera Expert Solutions Ltd; PublishDrive edition), May 2018

O Donaile, Lorcan, Podiatry Business Success Secrets: The Ultimate Guide to Building A Profitable Podiatry Practice That Works Without You, (Independently Published), Jan 2020

Websites

How to calculate business start up costs, British Business Bank, https://www.startuploans.co.uk/business-advice/how-to-calculate-business-start-costs/, 12/08/2021

How to stop feeling guilty about charging your patients, Private Practice Ninja, Dr Cath, https://www.privatepracticeninja.co.uk/stop-feeling-guilty-charging-patients/,12/10/21

Restaurant Owner's Fun Response to Reviewer Who Complained About the Price of Hot Water, Fine Dining Lovers, by Fine Dining Lovers, Editorial Staff, https://www.finedininglovers.com/article/restaurant-owners-fun-response-reviewer-who-complained-about-price-hot-water, 18/02/2021

Running a Business From Home: UK Laws, goselfemployed.co, Anita Forrest, https://goselfemployed.co/run-business-from-home/, 19/03/21

Chapter 4: Smart People Have A Successful Plan
Books

Doran, G.T, , Doran, G. T. (1981). There's a S.M.A.R.T. Way to Write Management's Goals and Objectives, Management Review, Vol. 70, Issue 11, pp. 35-36.

Drucker, Peter F, The Practice of Management, (New York : Harper & Row), 1954

Hogbin, Julie, Goal Setting - The Practical 'How To' Guide : for You, for Others, for Business, for Change (On Point Series for Conscious Leadership in Business & Life), (Independently published), Dec 2020

Websites

I built a start-up that makes up to $24,000 a month without a business plan — and I'm convinced you don't need one, either, Insider, Cat LeBlanc, https://www.businessinsider.com/business-plan-advice-startup-entrepreneurs-2018-5?r=US&IR=T, 24/03/21

dōTERRA MLM Review (2021): Selling the Sh*t Outta Essential Oils, The Economic Secretariat, Simon L Smith, https://www.ecosecretariat.org/doterra-mlm-review/, 7/10/21

How to write a business plan: step-by-step and business plan template download, Simply Business, Sam Bromley, https://www.simplybusiness.co.uk/knowledge/articles/2020/11/how-to-write-a-business-plan-template/, 24/03/21

Setting S.M.A.R.T.E.R. goals: 7 steps to achieving any goal, Wonderlust worker, https://www.wanderlustworker.com/setting-s-m-a-r-t-e-r-goals-7-steps-to-achieving-any-goal/, 11/08/21

Is there a difference between being self-employed and being a sole trader? Simply Business, Jade Wimbledon, https://www.simplybusiness.co.uk/knowledge/articles/2016/02/difference-between-self-employed-and-sole-trader/, 24/03/21

Chapter 5: Knowledgeable People Let Their Customers Find Them Easily
Book

Dib, Allen, The 1-Page Marketing Plan: Get New Customers, Make More Money, And Stand out From The Crowd, (Successwise), Jan 2015

Website

How to set a marketing budget for your small business, Ketchup marketing agency, Editorial, https://www.ketchup-marketing. co.uk/a-z-of-marketing/how-to-set-a-small-biz-marketing-budget/, 06/04/21

Chapter 6: Crazy People Want Things They Don't Need
Book

Melnupe, Gija, Pet Friendly Garden Design Guide, (Coffee Girl Designs), Jan 2020

Websites

10 great companies that started out selling something else, retire@21, Catherina Davey, https://retireat21.com/ entrepreneurship/10-companies-started-out-selling-something-else, 07/04/21

A Guide to Digital Business Cards in 2021, Hi Hello, Mel Chiri, https://www.hihello.me/blog/a-guide-to-digital-business-cards, 17/09/21

Near Field Communication Tag (NFC tag), techopedia, https://www.techopedia.com/definition/28812/near-field-communication-tag-nfc-tag, 17/09/21

QR Code Security: What are QR codes and are they safe to use?, Kasperkey, https://www.kaspersky.co.uk/resource-center/ definitions/what-is-a-qr-code-how-to-scan, 17/09/21

Top 10 things to remember when changing your company name, The company warehouse, Editorial, https://www. thecompanywarehouse.co.uk/blog/top-10-things-to-remember-when-changing-your-company-name, 07/04/21

Chapter 7: Wise People Ask For Help
Websites

Americans buy 11 billion paperclips a year, The Atlantic, Dino Grandoni, https://www.theatlantic.com/business/ archive/2011/08/americans-buy-11-billion-paper-clips-year/338575/, 7/10/21

What's the difference between a mentor and a coach? Small Business Trends, Shubhomita Bose, https://smallbiztrends.com/2016/02/difference-mentor-coach.html#:~:text=Mentoring%20is%20a%20 long%2Dterm,more%20structured%20and%20formal%20 approach, 07/04/21

Chapter 8: People Who Learn The Business Dance Find New Connections
Book

Adey, Ladey, Successful Business Networking Online: Increase your Marketing, Leadership and Entrepreneurship through Online Connections, (Ladey Adey Publications), Sept 2020, Revised Edition Oct 2021

Websites

Buehner, Carl W, , Buehner was quoted as saying, "They may forget what you said — but they will never forget how you made them feel." in Richard Evans' Quote Book, a 1971 compilation of quotations of prominent figures in the LDS church. This quote is often misattributed to many others including Maya Angelou. https://en.wikipedia.org/wiki/Carl_W._Buehner

Social Network Usage & Growth Statistics: How Many People Use Social Media in 2021?, Backlink, Brian Dean, https://backlinko.com/social-media-users, 08/04/21

Chapter 9: Clever People Develop Good Habits
Books

Sutton Johal, Karen, The 4 Money Mindsets, (Writing Matters Publishing), Aug 2016

Warren, Elizabeth, Warren Tyagi, Amelia, All Your Worth: The Ultimate Lifetime Money Plan, (Freepress), Mar 2005

Websites

How to Deal With FOMO in Your Life, verywellmind, Elizabeth Scott, MS, https://www.verywellmind.com/how-to-cope-with-fomo-4174664, 15/04/21

How to Raise Prices for Existing Customers, CXL, Derek Gleason, https://cxl.com/blog/how-to-raise-prices/, 7-10-21

Chapter 10: Shrewd People Manage Their Time Effectively
Book

Briant, Penny, How to create more time for you & live an amazing life.: Coaching for women, (Independently Published), Sept 2018

Websites

Calculating your IGA, Progressive Property, https://www.progressiveproperty.co.uk/calculating-your-iga/#:~:text=Make%20sure%20that%20all%20income,%2C%20on%20average%2C%20%C2%A3x., 21/09/21

Why giving away free services can smash your brand, LinkedIn, Sue Parker, https://www.linkedin.com/pulse/why-giving-away-free-services-always-good-idea-sue-parker/, 15/04/21

Performance Management – Goals, Objectives, KRAs, KPIs – What's the Difference?, Talent Align OD, https://www.talentalign.com/knowledgebase/performance-management-goals-objectives-kras-kpis-whats-the-difference-2/, 17/09/21

Chapter 11: Healthy People Manage Their Physical Health

Book

Conley, Rosemary, Morris, Mary, The 28-Day Immunity Plan: A vital diet and fitness plan to boost resilience and protect your health, (Penguin), Jan 2021

Websites

Part 3: Adult overweight and obesity, NHSdigital, https://digital.nhs.uk/data-and-information/publications/statistical/statistics-on-obesity-physical-activity-and-diet/england-2020/part-3-adult-obesity-copy, 16/04/21

Seasonal affective disorder (SAD), MayoClinic, Clinic staff, https://www.mayoclinic.org/diseases-conditions/seasonal-affective-disorder/symptoms-causes/syc-20364651#:~:text=Seasonal%20affective%20disorder%20(SAD)%20is,and%20making%20you%20feel%20moody., 16/04/21

Where's the line when mixing alcohol and business?, Entrepreneurhandbook, Editorial, https://entrepreneurhandbook.co.uk/mixing-alcohol-and-business/, 16/04/21

Chapter 12: Healthy People Manage Their Mental Health

Books

Dispenza, Dr. Joe, Becoming Supernatural, (Freepress), Jan 2006

Gilad, Sandy, The Instant Switch, (Sandy Gilad), 2015

Godley, Elaine, My Right Breast Used to be My Stomach: Until Cancer Moved It, Mar 2013

Palmer, Rosalyn, Reset!: A blueprint for a better life, (Panoa Press), Sept 2018

Rose, Nicola, Echoes of The Moon, (Independently Published), May 2021

Sheldon, Christie Marie, Love or Above, https://www.mindvalley.com/christie-marie-sheldon/love-or-above/, (Mindvalley).

Whitehead, Lisa, Get a Life! - The Guide Book, (John Hunt Publishing), Nov 2012

Websites

6 Psychological Reasons Why You Take Things Too Personally, Medium, Nick Wignall, https://medium.com/simple-pub/6-psychological-reasons-why-you-take-things-too-personally-6c46c21402a1, 16/04/21

Moving from Blame to Accountability, TheSystemsThinker, Marilyn Paul, https://thesystemsthinker.com/moving-from-blame-to-accountability/, 16/04/21

The life changing inventions the experts said were impossible, News.Com.au, Nick Wigham, https://www.entrepreneur.com/article/251290, 16/04/21

Thinking about the past and future in daily life: an experience sampling study of individual differences in mental time travel, Springer Link, Roger E. Beaty1 · Paul Seli2 · Daniel L. Schacter3, https://scholar.harvard.edu/files/schacterlab/files/beatyselischacter_psychologicalresearch_2019.pdf, 16/09/21

Your Words Have Impact, So Think Before You Speak, EntrepreneurEurope, Matt Mayberry, https://www.entrepreneur.com/article/251290#:~:text=Each%20word%20that%20we%20use%20can%20have%20a%20colossal%20impact.&text=Words%20influence%20others%20and%20build,whether%20it's%20good%20or%20bad., 16/04/21

About the Author

Melanie is a qualified Foot Health Practitioner, Speaker and Trainer at one of the UK's top business training academies.

Writing this book was certainly a challenge but Melanie was determined to share her experience of moving from a securely paid job to having her own business with no knowledge on running or managing a business. She gives practical advice to absolute beginners in business keeping in mind people who are coming from a similar background to her when she started her business.

Melanie has completed countless business courses over the past years and realised when writing this book she had actually learnt something from them!

She hopes a little bit of her humour comes through in the book and you find it insightful and enjoyable to read. She says her next book, which she is in the process of downloading from her head, will be much easier to write than this one!

Melanie currently lives with 2 cats and a husband. The cats allow her and her husband to keep the garden tidy for them and she finds pulling weeds to be quite cathartic although the weeds seem to grow quicker than she can pull them up.

Coming out of a toxic job made Melanie reassess her own health and has learned running a business highlights how vulnerable you are if you are not looking after your health. This has included her using and learning more about essential oils, meditating and taking daily walks and exercise.

Welcome to The Happy Foot Clinic

thehappyfootclinic.com

Contact Melanie:
thehappyfootclinic@gmail.com

Regular newsletter sent out - just ask to be part of my tribe.

Other Websites

dōTERRA business)
mydoterra.com/thehappyfootclinic/#/

Enagic machine business
kangenwaterhwh.com/

Facebook
www.facebook.com/TheHappyFootClinic/

LinkedIn
www.linkedin.com/in/melanie-smith-rawlings-038b1433/

Twitter
twitter.com/happyfootclinic?lang=en

YouTube
youtube.com/channel/UCzpTIzQ3tknyPJv85DI-NAQ

www.fromjobtoboss.com/
gives access to extra resources from this book or Scan Me to reach the page.

Index

Endorsements

"If you're thinking of taking the leap of faith and launching your own business, then this wonderfully crafted guide shares all the steps to success.

Melanie shares from her own first hand experience, which brings the reader priceless nuggets of wisdom, from someone who has personally walked the path and learnt from both the highs and the lows of the journey of becoming a business owner."

Lisa Davies, Chief Inspiration Officer,
Get the Edge Training & Consultancy

"I wish that this book had been around when I took the leap of faith transitioning from employment to starting my own business initially as a reflexologist and complementary therapist many years ago.

This book is a great resource for anyone who has a desire to start their own business as well as being a successful business entrepreneur whilst living a healthy and fulfilled life.

Melanie has certainly walked the walk and shares with the reader many learnings, lived experiences and top tips to inform, inspire and support the reader in doing just that with her unique informative, pragmatic and humorous approach and style of writing.

I am sure this signature book created by Melanie, is the first of many more to come, as she travels through life positively impacting on and helping many others as they start and then create their own exciting entrepreneurial journey in life."

Sharon Griffiths (aka The Curious Connector),
Published author with *World Game Changer books*, **lifelong learner and educator, entrepreneur and property investor**

"Wherever you are you can only start from that position, the past will help and hinder you. One thing is for sure you have the present to create your own future - make your time count as Melanie has done and is doing - everything is possible with a vision, a plan and action."

Julie Hogbin, Human Behaviourist,
Founder: Clavemglobal

"So you've been thinking about starting your own well-being business for a while but just haven't got around to taking that first step? It's not unusual to have to face your fears to take that first step - so, if you're going to make that decision, why learn the hard way yourself when someone is offering you their learning experiences (some people call them mistakes) to learn from? This book will save you lots of stress, help you get clarity on what you really want and how you're going to go about it. So what are you waiting for? Get reading and crack on."

Kerry Malster, Business Coach @ ActionCOACH

"I've known Melanie for several years and her passion for learning and self-development has been key to her growth. It's been great to see her increase in confidence and move from having a JOB to being a successful business owner and accomplished speaker.

Melanie's book outlines how she built her business and is an essential 'warts and all' account of her journey, packed with top tips and her indomitable humour for those wishing to do the same. "

Hayley Meakes, Marketer, Mentor, Speaker
and Founder of SnipBit Podcast

"NOW more than ever before we are in need of faith, encouragement and guidance for our life and business. 2020 and 2021 has brought some home truths and perhaps a motivation to change. If it's you — this book will help you achieve what you had set out and more. Step by step guidance to understanding a business, it's principles and rules of success, written by a business owner who once stood right where you are right now. Designed for businesses in the health industry – loved by everyone who dares to make a change."

Gija Melnupe, Landscape Designer,
Coffee Girl Designs

"So you think any idiot can run a business? Melanie humourously explores how it actually takes a very special type of idiot; skilfully guiding you though her experiences of navigating the shark infested waters of self-employment to running a small business start-up. It is the best beginners guide to what is REALLY involved in transitioning from Employed to Entrepreneur! This is the book which teaches you everything they didn't teach you in school! With focus on business diversity, self worth, survival and most importantly self care, this is the book I wish had existed 20 years ago when I started my own Private Practice Podiatry Clinic!

It should be included on the essential reading list for anyone who's ever considered leaving employed Heathcare to take on their own business! Nicola O'Brian, Podiatrist, Healthcare Business Coach and one of those special types of 'idiot'."

Nicola O'Brian BSc (Hons) Pod, HCPC Reg,
RCOP, MInstCP, AssRCM,
CEO Love Your Feet Ltd **and LYF Training.**

"Melanie is an absolute angel, her passion, knowledge, experience, and her willingness to progress and support others is inspiring and importantly her desire and passion to work on herself which is key in life and impacts every other aspect of life is amazing. Seeing Melanie grow and watch her on this journey has been an absolute delight and I am excited to see what happens with her and her business and that will evolve is supporting others on this journey."

I for one know how taking that leap of faith can feel exciting and anxious. With the right support, guidance you will be thankful you did it and Melanie's knowledge will most certainly help get you there.

Nicola Rose, *Creative Well-Being Pathways*

"Some people wish they could tell their boss to stuff it and leave a job they hate. Very few actually do. This is a book is by a lady who did!

This is a great read for anyone wanting to leave a job they hate. Melanie covers the real highs and the real lows in a very amusing way and helps you understand why you too should take that leap.

There is lots of practical information, about how to handle and how not to handle, the numerous new and challenging situations you will encounter. This is so important because if this is the first time you're starting your business, you don't know what you don't know. A great read!"

Karen Sutton-Johal, *Investor and Business Builder. Author*

"Every day I meet people who either have or are thinking about the leap from Employment to Self-Employment. People with an incredible talent in their chosen profession but realising there is so much more to being their own boss than they first thought. This book is a wonderful guide to help anyone find their own way, giving fantastic tips, a great insight to what to expect and if you can what to avoid.

Don't let the unknown stop you following your dream, let Melanie and her wonderful book be the inspiration and information you need."

Johanna Thompson, Founder: *The Wellness Network*

"What is it that I can say that will make a difference an impact for anyone looking to read this amazing brilliance by the lovely Melanie? This book is a stepping stone for all who are starting out in business and have no idea where to start.

The book has knowledge, know-how and the wisdom from a true soul perspective and through Melanie's own experience. It will guide and inspire you with truth that is relateable."

Suzie Welstead, _Emotional Well-Being Coach_

Boxes for your notes, on this and subsequent pages. As you read, write down here how you are going to implement your learning for your business.

Your notes.

Your notes.

Your notes.

Your notes.

Your notes.

Your notes.

Your notes.

Your notes.

9 781913 579289